Secular and Spiritual Values

Educational debate in the western world is currently dominated by pragmatic, utilitarian values. The prevailing assumption is that education should be geared towards fitting people into the world of work. Dudley Plunkett breaks new ground in this debate by seeking to reconcile secular and spiritual values in educational policy and practice.

Secular and Spiritual Values presents a critique of the influence of enterprise culture on education. It argues that the resurgence of interest in the spiritual today represents a return to an essential aspect of human nature, and maintains that the spiritual perspective can provide a context for the regeneration of values in education. It indicates a way forward which, while not denying pragmatism, rationalism or holistic values, calls for openness to a spiritual reality that is seen as primary. It also assesses the practical implications and priorities for action if education is to contribute to the exploration of the spiritual as well as the intellectual and emotional dimensions of human experience.

This book has grown out of the author's twenty-five years' experience in educational studies, and from his particular preoccupation with values in education. It should interest those concerned with the nature and purpose of education: teachers, parents, educational policy-makers and administrators and academics in the field.

The Author
Dudley Plunkett is Senior Lecturer in Education at the University of Southampton.

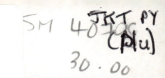

Secular and Spiritual Values

Grounds for Hope in Education

Dudley Plunkett

Routledge
London and New York

First published 1990
by Routledge
11 New Fetter Lane, London EC4P 4EE

Simultaneously published in the USA and Canada
by Routledge
a division of Routledge, Chapman and Hall, Inc.
29 West 35th Street, New York, NY 10001

Typeset by LaserScript Limited, Mitcham, Surrey
Printed and bound in Great Britain by Mackays of Chatham PLC, Chatham, Kent

British Library Cataloguing in Publication Data

Plunkett, Dudley
Secular and spiritual values: grounds for hope in education.
1. Education. Values
I. Title
370.11 ISBN 0-415-03508-2

Library of Congress Cataloging in Publication Data
Plunkett, Dudley.
  Secular and spiritual values : grounds for hope in education / Dudley
Plunkett.
    p. cm.
  Includes bibliographical references.
  ISBN 0-415-03508-2
  1. Education—Aims and objectives. 2. Values—Study and teaching.
  3. Educational sociology. I. Title.
  LB41.P67 1990
  370.11—dc20
                                                                89–39166
                                                                   CIP

SB 40798 /30 · 7·90

Contents

Contents

Preface

The intention of this book is one that justifies a preliminary word, partly of warning, partly of reassurance. The warning relates to what the book is not. It is not a theological, still less a confessional work. Nor does it attempt to treat the notion of the spiritual as broadly as that term is used by writers from many different perspectives today. Specifically, I do not take a relativist view of the spiritual. Had I chosen not to endorse any particular belief about the nature of the spiritual, that would be tantamount to a relativist option which would imply inviting the reader to do the same. My argument, however, is that the mind can be open without having to be empty, and that it is more fruitful to engage with each other in terms of values, beliefs and commitments that we actually hold, than to set these aside for fear of disrespect towards those of other persuasions.

On the other hand, there is much common ground to be explored in values, beliefs and commitments in the educational field, and the book has an intent which is ecumenical, in the largest sense. All those who have a sense of the transcendence of spiritual being and power are involved in such reflection about the nature and purpose of education, for they will be painfully aware of how widespread the subordination of education to material and political interests has become. Indeed, work of much wider scope than this is needed, extending beyond education and challenging the secular/spiritual divide that rationalist thinking has imposed on the modern world, whether East, West or urbanized South.

The hopefulness of this work signalled in its title lies in the signs that can be detected of efforts to reclaim the wholeness, even the holiness, of education, and indeed of civilization. Although here I can aim at little more than the opening up of a very neglected agenda, naming some of its themes and potentials, the possibility of a more substantial exploration to be shared by many is already evident. What is required is to step into the spiritual dimension, not in such a way as to ignore secular considerations, but to transcend their limitations.

This proposal may shock, but consider this: the spiritual, about which this book sets out to speak, is ineffable. At the very least it is not amenable to purely rational analysis. The most scholarly treatment of the subject could not be as valuable as personal experience and insight, sharing directly with others, and living a life committed to spiritual values. The spiritual is that part of life which holds its mystery, and always will. Reason is not eroding the territory of the spiritual. We will never understand rationally the characteristic paradoxes of the spiritual life: of strength in weakness, freedom in service, completion in self-sacrifice, and life in death. The conclusions one reaches from reflecting on such themes may be binding, but not in logic, and their discovery is always a personal one.

So while the experience of preparing this book will, as is conventional, scarcely obtrude in the following pages, it has been essential and determining. The writing of a book can be a truer message than its text. This book comes out of a particular, and therefore limited, experience of teaching, of personal exchange, and of insights found in seeking a way of living. As in so many works, the printed words on the page are merely a relic of the writer's experience. But when writing about the spiritual this is even more the case, because the words were never more than a relic of the experience, even for the writer. The corollary of this is that the work can only hope to be a stimulus to the reader to seek his or her own awareness of the spiritual; it cannot pass on any conclusions that do not match with the reader's own experience. The book stands as a mediator of the common experience of writer and reader, and, in the case of a work aiming to reflect upon the spiritual dimension of life, can only fulfil its task if both are open to each other's insights, whatever their individual starting-points.

I have greatly appreciated the interest and helpfulness of others that have gone into the making of this book. Some whom I might have mentioned would be very surprised, but I owe a particular debt to Roy Wake for his inspiration and commitment in making values a central issue of educational practice and policy, and to Brian Hill who gave me thoughtful guidance in the closing stages of my work. I also thank my family for the strength they have given me, and especially Francine, my wife.

Dudley Plunkett
Southampton University

Part one

Issues and concerns

Introduction

When a speaker at a conference referred to spiritual values in his talk, the chairperson, a reputed moral philosopher, interjected: 'Tell me a spiritual value that is not a moral value'. The reply came instantly: 'Holiness'. In the silence that followed this exchange I felt all the tension which underlies this book. Either we are indulging in a semantic exercise or there are fundamentally distinct understandings of reality that are not going to be rationally harmonized. Put plainly, if the chairperson was right, then talk of holiness, or any appeal to a knowledge that cannot be turned into a more fully explicated understanding, is mere illusion. But if the speaker was right, and there is a knowledge of which reason is only a quite minor part, then most of us have indeed betrayed our birthright for pottage. And they cannot both be right!

The spiritual dimension of human experience has virtually disappeared from the repertoire of contemporary writers about education. There is a gap in the literature which cannot be made good by returning to classical sources. Little has been written in this century about those spiritual needs of western society that can to some degree be met by education. The tradition that recognizes non-rational modes of knowing has always been part of western culture, and of the Jewish tradition before that, and has now gone down an ever-increasing number of psychological and psychic by-ways. The view that there can be no spiritual life if God is dead, or treated as if he were, provides a perspective on education, as indeed on the whole of life, that deserves at least as serious a hearing as the materialist and modern metaphysical theories which are in any case so often mutually contradictory.

Any statement made on these massive themes must be made from a particular standpoint of commitment, and in humility; otherwise it is irrelevant and inadequate. This is because what is being discussed is strictly speaking ineffable: it cannot be confined by logical, rational discourse because it is concerned with a different dimension of reality.

The task will therefore be to refer as authentically as possible to a domain of experience and belief, so as to hint at the possibility of a radical change in social and educational priorities, but without falling into the trap of treating this simply as a rational problem-solving exercise. The spiritual faculty generates a knowledge, not of causes and explanations, but of meanings and purposes which can inspire, reconcile and unify values and interests. And it can scarcely be denied that western societies and their educational systems are in desperate need of the values of hope, joy, peace, love, reverence and holiness that the spiritual perspective reveals.

This book has been stimulated, even provoked, by the fact that pragmatism, the opposite of spirituality, is currently in the political ascendancy. A statement of protest, of the kind at which the book aims, is vitally needed if both the secular curriculum and the spiritual dimension of education are not to be further subjected to the short-term political expediency of current legislation in Britain and similar policies in other self-assuredly 'advanced' western societies. The taken-for-grantedness of secular materialist values, culminating in a morally anarchic individualism, needs to be challenged for its eroding influence upon what education can contribute to maintaining civilized humanity.

The tension between a pragmatic view of education, as the means to political and economic ends, and a contrasting vision of learning, as the continuous refinement of meaning, engages all learners, teachers and parents, as well as all others who administer and govern the educational system. It might seem that it would be desirable to reach agreement about our educational values, one way or the other, and thus terminate their unending discussion. But what would that solve? Pragmatic solutions would surely end in a quagmire of warring political interests, as we so clearly see at present, while contemplative views could leave educational practice in the state of physical and mental paralysis for which its theoreticians are so often taunted.

For the time being, then, the tension must be faced, and we must explore the various conceivable ways forward as honestly and fairly as can be achieved. One possible outcome, which is the rational approach, is to analyse the terms, to seek to clarify the debate, to identify the policies that are being proposed, and to pursue the enquiry as a theoretical and practical problem. This solution is the one that has most adherents in the academic and professional worlds, and if I devote only one chapter exclusively to it (Chapter three), it must nevertheless pervade much of the rest of the book which is constrained by its very nature to follow certain rules of logical order and rationality.

An alternative way forward is much more difficult to convey in written form, but my hope is that it will emerge gradually from the book as a whole. It will be argued that the rational marks a step forward from the pragmatic, but this does not prevent us looking beyond the rational, something we can do in two stages. The first of these (in Chapter four) is to see education as the development not just of the thinking powers of learners but of their whole personalities. This is referred to below as the holistic view of education, though many would say that this is what education should be anyway, and that the qualifying word 'holistic' should be unnecessary. I believe that it is justified because a truly holistic treatment of education requires us to see educational questions as merely part of a much vaster range of psychological, sociological, political and ecological problems and concerns, and to seek to balance our understanding and appreciation of human needs and potentials by reference to their global context and significance. Be that as it may, we are a long way from seeing holistic education pervade our national education systems in the western world.

The undefined spiritual dimension

But even this education of the whole personality in the physical and social setting is incomplete, I will contend. If we were just considering educational methods it might not be necessary to go on to a further stage (in Chapter five) to look at education in spiritual terms. We have a sufficient choice of methods. But if we ask why one method of education rather than another, and if we see that it all depends on what kind of person or what kind of society we prefer, then we engage in a new set of questions that are not addressed by anything that I have said so far. A recent document published by the British Department of Education and Science (1987), *The National Curriculum 5–16: a Consultation Document*, several times used the word 'secular' to describe the school curriculum. The word jars because either it means nothing at all, and could be omitted, or it is distinguishing the proposed curriculum from a non-secular curriculum, which is nowhere described or even identified. The 1988 Education Reform Act uses the term 'spiritual' in relation to the curriculum, and this presumably refers to its non-secular dimensions; however, spiritual is not defined. Yet I think that the framers of the 1988 legislation are unwittingly pointing their finger at a major gap in modern education: the lack of an articulated moral and spiritual foundation to reform plans. This book could be seen as a response to this situation. I see the spiritual dimension of education as a potential fusion of energies, of pupils, parents, teachers, administrators and policy-makers, in some common purpose, a purpose that is very rarely even looked for in official documents, and one which has certainly never been clearly and deliberately expressed.

Does such a purpose matter, if it is so little referred to and appears to many to be obscure? It is only necessary to recognize the lack of involvement of so many learners, the frustration of parents, the divided loyalties of teachers, and the desperation of politicians, to see that there is no peace possible in education without a new kind of questioning by all involved, a questioning that looks *within* for meaning and purpose rather than seeking to impose ready-made solutions on others. The intent of this book is to contribute to such an enquiry. If this obliges me to be severe in judgement at times, and at others to adopt views myself that may seem no less vulnerable, I see this as just part of a dialogue that can continue. A book is no substitute for a conversation, or perhaps it is only to be justified as part of a very long-term conversation.

In the alternative mode of enquiry being proposed, beyond recognizing the need for an education of the whole personality, we need to explore the spiritual dimension of education. The spiritual, in this context, is taken as referring to the sensing of a unifying meaning and purpose for education. The reference in the title of this book to spiritual values partly reflects the historical reality that our western civilization was once much clearer than it is now about the ultimate purposes of education, indeed about the purposes of life as a whole. Although I shall not argue that the solution to modern questions about meaning lies in turning back to the past, I do acknowledge that my own beliefs and values are formed in continuity with a past from which I am still able to draw inspiration. In any case, it seems self-evident that we cannot adequately explore the spiritual dimension at second hand, but that we must draw upon our own reflections and lived experience.

If this seems to set up a tension between the rational and the experiential, then that could be just a further manifestation of the central issue of the anecdote with which I began. We need both reason and experience, but we can easily betray our experience by being always willing to yield to reason. What I therefore try to do in this book is to point to the places where, as I see it, reason has to yield to experience. The experience includes that of everyday practical living, of people, of teaching, of problems in life, and of the development of personal beliefs and values. Out of this experience comes a truth that is admittedly personal, but which is more important than reason, because it provides meaning, purpose and direction which reason alone cannot give. Inevitably, then, the rational and the experiential will jockey for position here as elsewhere. There is no other way to address the core of the topic of this book, because we betray it if we deal with it in an exclusively rational way.

It appears to me that it is essential that work of this kind is now done in education, and not simply by professionals. Twenty-five years in educational research and teaching seem to have brought me to a major cross-roads, and I suspect I am like many others in acknowledging that I am having to change my mind from how I used to see things (Plunkett and Lynch, 1973). I cannot follow official thinking about education with any conviction at all, and I see no luminaries, no prophets, who are guiding me in directions which I can identify rationally or experientially as entirely adequate. Yet I believe wholeheartedly that we can cultivate our minds, develop our personalities, and search for meaning and value in experience, and that it is through what we call education that such possibilities exist for most in the western world.

When we look at the history of Europe we see countless errors of humanity, and all the inhumanity, but we can also see the vision of truth that inspired so many artists, writers, architects, statesmen and saints. We cannot go back to mediaeval Europe, but we can see one feature of those times that held everything together, and which is largely lacking from the contemporary world, the belief that there was a unifying purpose to life (Jaki, 1978; Capra, 1983). This, then is my starting-point. In the service of a unifying purpose to life, I would like to ask how far education is serving such a purpose, and under what circumstances and by what means it might better do so.

It will at once be asked: what might be such a unifying purpose? If all were agreed upon this, then there would be no problem of values. Inevitably, this will be the most contentious element of my approach. However, it is surely only by being sympathetic to others' efforts to comprehend that we can learn from each other and find a mutually acceptable way forward, and so I hope that what I have to say will be accepted as part of a process of honest searching. Although I believe in an ultimate truth, I do not imagine that I or any of my readers fully possess it. We may be searching, or we may believe we are approaching our goal, but we are all in light and shadow. We can, however, enlighten one another, communicating with each other through reason and experience.

The greatest gift to our society and to its educational system would be one of hope. Starting from hope there can be regeneration. But hope has to have a source. This book is aimed at searching for sources of, and ways of grounding, hope, and I am confident that this search will not be a fruitless one. To find hope, we must first recognize our need for it, that is we must recognize our mistakes in the lack of sense of direction and even destructiveness of much modern educational practice. This means that we need to be critical of what exists. Such criticism, however, does not need to become negative, vindictive, personalized, or contemptuous. We have all made the same mistakes. We have all followed the fashions, allowed ourselves to become absorbed by our enthusiasms, myopic in our zeal, unappreciative of the contributions of those who were starting from different premises.

Although dealing with a topic that is not encompassable in rational terms, as will appear especially in the later chapters, the book does proceed by a succession of identifiable steps. Chapter one provides a suggested map and panoramic view of alternative value perspectives and suggests some of the issues they pose for education. Chapters two to five discuss the value alternatives in greater detail within the social and educational context of western society. Broadly, the alternatives are: the market economy, or pragmatic model (Chapter two); the rational–scientific models which aspire to being demonstrably valid (Chapter three); holistic models which recognize the relevance of more comprehensive understandings of human personality and experience (Chapter four); and spiritual understandings which attach universal and religious significance to human awareness and behaviour (Chapter five). The last two chapters offer a synthesis of the elements now needed in a strategy of educational regeneration (Chapter six), and an appraisal of the practical implications and priorities for action (Chapter seven), if education is to contribute fruitfully to the exploration not only of the intellectual, but also of the affective and spiritual dimensions of human experience.

Chapter one

Society and education: a crisis of values

Michael Ignatieff: How is it that a writer remains engaged with...what is going on out there in a world which is, in lots of ways...very repellent and very frightening?
Saul Bellow: I don't know why I care about it, that's one of these questions that leads you to, into theology. But I do. And what a writer like me is apt to feel is that in all this moronic inferno... there is some loss of the power to experience life.

(Bourne *et al.*, 1987: 25)

There is a long-running and worldwide debate about whether educational systems can only reflect society, or should be thought of as one of the means by which society finds its way forward into the unknown future. Some would say that schools are constrained to follow society, largely because they depend upon public support, both moral and financial, and that their proper concern is not society at large but the specific task of developing scarce talent and needed skills among the young. In contrast, it is argued that, by raising the consciousness of individuals and groups in society, schools can bring benefits which are not necessarily calculable in advance. And so values polarize and the argument see-saws, while the whole educational enterprise seems to drift directionlessly, with teachers and schools criticized simultaneously for failing to conform to enduring expectations and for not providing solutions to society's evolving problems.

Values are relatively stable choices or preferences about how to be or to behave and, in relation to education, concern what it is considered education should achieve. Value positions may be adopted unreflectingly, and thus be no different from prejudices, or they may be the product of rational and experiential enquiry leading to or from deeply-held beliefs. The truth of values is not provable, since it rests upon basic assumptions, but such assumptions can be exposed to examination and criticism. Anyone who sets out, as I am doing, to examine the values of others is obliged to pay equal attention to their own, and to be as forthright as possible in so doing. We all have the awesome freedom of deciding which values and beliefs count most for us, and therefore we are responsible for our decisions and for our failures to decide.

Five aspects of the crisis

The crisis of values we confront in educational institutions and in the wider society is a real one, and it is deepening. This theme could easily be the subject of a book in itself, but my purpose here is confined to outlining five propositions highlighting aspects of the values crisis which I see as central in considering the future role of education in western society.

Proposition 1: Rising levels of personal and social aggression are undermining human relationships.

This is the most radical proposition, since it affects everyone. Unless we close our eyes to aggression by privatizing our existences, or else cloak our view of social reality in self-justifying and unexamined ideologies, we cannot fail to be jarred by the sense that human society is undergoing major disruptions. At both personal and communal levels, this virtually pathological state, to which Saul Bellow refers as 'the moronic inferno', shows itself in three main ways. First, fierce reactions to threat, whether real or imagined, express themselves ideologically in such forms as sectarianism, neo-fascism, racism and sexism. Such ideologies are explicit all around us in daily life, whether brazenly or in self-righteous disguise. We can see them, for example, in the political struggle in Northern Ireland, in New Right movements in Britain and throughout Western Europe (Cochrane and Billig, 1982), and in racially motivated urban riots in Europe and the United States. Second, there are survival strategies which are mainly interpersonal, which find expression in much juvenile crime and physical violence, though there can be an ideological or socially induced protest element in some cases of vandalism, such as in schools, that stem at least in part from a sense of injustice (HMI, 1987; Emler and Reicher, 1987).

And, third, there is the more passive, but no less pathological reaction of dropping out, of forming marginalized and often counter- culture groups with alternative lifestyles, usually associated with the use of addictive substances which equates to a kind of psychological, and sometimes physical self-destruction. Indeed, suicides of under-twenty-fives have increased by a quarter in the last decade in Britain, and now form almost one tenth of all suicides. Progressively more alienated behaviours of this kind represent a form of violence in society, though it may not always be clear who is at their source. Opportunities denied to young people or to minorities, especially for employment or political participation, can produce the marginalization phenomenon, as do particular groups' assumptions of superiority over members of another group, creed, class, or even age cohort. There is an unmistakable note of blaming that is widespread in society, where the target changes from police to government, to minorities, to youth, to homosexuals, to teachers. This blaming reaction acts as a self-fulfilling prophecy, in that it ensures that it becomes less and less possible to see positive qualities or human value behind the stereotyped labels.

All these reactions threaten the fundamental contract that underlies human social life. Why then do they happen? It is plain that the phenomena and their causes are as much sociological in character as psychological. That is to say that, although they undoubtedly reflect personal and moral viewpoints or decisions, they are influenced by a variety of social structures and forces. The first proposition, then, depends in considerable measure upon macrosocial conditions.

Proposition 2: The most publicly vaunted values work against the conditions needed for peaceful co-existence on the planet.

There is a widespread sense of cynicism and drift in our everyday view of the state of the world. This is summed up in the recurrent polarities of news reports: East–West, North–South, left–right, rich–poor, black–white, multilateral–unilateral. The significant fact about these pairs of concepts is that they define one another. They are essentially reactive rather than pro-active, and they are artificially manufactured rather than reflecting actual experiences and encounters. Young people growing up under such stimuli encounter a make-believe world, one that is pre-digested and mechanistic. Only in the context of such inert ideas could anyone really envisage the nuclear destruction of the other half of the planet, the acceptance of an annual total of deaths from starvation equal to more than the entire population of Australia, or the irreversible erosion of our ecosystem out of short-term economic calculation.

It is not valid to argue that these critical events are out of our hands. We all help to sustain the economic and political systems whose materialism, prodigal exploitation, feebleness of purpose and uncaringness express very precisely what we are prepared to tolerate, even if we do not consciously advocate what is happening. The alienation and protest of the young may be irrational responses to the economic and political environment, but they are psychologically comprehensible. To what extent, then, do we seek to counter such conditioning in the way we educate the young?

Proposition 3: Formal education is persistently inflexible and unresponsive to people's changing needs.

What has happened to people to make the world so different from what the vast majority must surely wish? And what happens to people so that they feel cut off from how the world is organized? The answer to these questions, tragically, is education. This is not to say schooling alone, but the subjection to all the influences upon human beings as they emerge into society, including child-rearing, systems of law and order, media exposure, membership of social, political, religious and other organizations, and working life: in short, all the processes of socialization that give us both our social identity and the conventional freedoms and constraints that accompany it.

Formal education in schools is, however, a major aspect of socialization, and also one that is potentially among the most accessible to public efforts at deliberate change. In what sense, then, has formal education been inflexible and unresponsive? Education has been relied upon to support parents and established society in reproducing the succeeding generation in their image. It is a relatively new idea, one that is more common in developing societies, that education could promote social change. The economic contribution of schooling, for example during the industrial revolution, was concerned with reinforcing rather than transforming society. Thus, most Western European societies are now reaping the results of having constructed protected and apolitical educational systems, for schools respond slowly to outside changes while remaining compulsive about their own internal rituals and preoccupations.

Not surprisingly, formal educational systems are now the subject of increasing controversy. In Britain especially, this debate has severely sharpened in the 1980s with the emergence of a strongly instrumentalist government educational policy, emphasizing such values as industry, competitiveness and self-reliance. In curricular terms this has meant a growing concentration upon vocationally useful knowledge and skills, especially in preparing the way for applications of the new technologies and for the selection of talent into occupations that promise to contribute to wealth-creation and to a politically stable society. An alternative view of education, which developed throughout the 1970s, envisaged curriculum reforms as being aimed primarily at meeting personal and social needs. Its priorities could be termed holistic, that is, balancing cognitive, emotional and moral dimensions of education, and seeing individuals as responsible for their own learning and participation in the development of the wider community.

Thus, schools have come under criticism from the right and left of the political spectrum. They are held accountable for economic failures of society through the lack of workers or managers with a satisfactory foundation of useful skills and knowledge, and they are blamed for the breakdown of the social and moral order and the stifling of qualities of imagination, creativity and compassion. They are called upon to solve the problems of unemployment, on the one hand, and Aids, drugs and football hooliganism, on the other.

Proposition 4: Educational reforms are needed that will nurture both individual consciousness and social development.

It is obvious that educational reform in schools, which western societies seem agreed is needed, must mean more than additions and subtractions of factual or theoretical curriculum content. It is the educational process itself that needs to be transformed so that it affects not only individuals' economic futures but their consciousness and their social development. Because educational reforms of this kind have never been widely attempted, the real importance of teachers and curriculum-builders has always been underestimated. What is needed from teachers is that they re-examine the present realities of education: What is its purpose, long-term as well as short-term? What values currently inform it, and what are their implications for curriculum and teaching? And how well do the outcomes of education meet its intentions? In so far as this re-appraisal leaves teachers feeling dissatisfied, frustrated or challenged, they face a task of educational transformation. What is most likely is that many teachers already recognize clearly that their work is fundamentally unproductive precisely because it is avoiding the central value issues, and this out of misgivings about putting professional security at risk and having to face public scrutiny and controversy.

Judged against the need, the task of education is vast, but also quite essential as part of society's efforts to surmount its crisis of values. Much of what passes for education ignores this task completely, and is only a static form of training. The true potential of education depends primarily upon the awareness, commitment and intentions of teachers in a task of personal and cultural transformation. It is also true that, while teachers have a central and indispensable role in the cultural nurture and consciousness-raising of the younger members of society, it is one they share with parents, teacher-educators, educational policy-makers and others.

Proposition 5: Everybody counts as a valuable participant in decisions being taken about values.

It is conceivable that education could seek to foster in each person a positive view of self, of community, of mankind, and of society's potential for further development. Such positive valuing of people and their viewpoints and qualities has, however, been widely disregarded in most western educational systems. Not only is personal respect an inalienable human right, but change, creativity and imagination emerge spontaneously when people feel themselves valued and participating. A greater reliance upon spontaneity in education need not, however, mean rejecting all the already-known needs of learners and society. These still need to be considered, but not as rigid and limiting targets.

Put another way, education as a process is capable of drawing out much more than what we have consciously packed into established science and culture. A rational approach, however, is not enough. Everyone involved needs the freedom to speak from their own moral and spiritual commitments and experiences. In this sense, everybody can be made to count, because we cannot assume that we know anyone's full potential before they have had a chance to participate. These ideas, radical as they are each time they are stated, are as old as education itself; they simply demand of education, as of society, its own constant renewal in the service of the human person.

These five propositions describe a crisis in society and education, and indicate some of the directions in which solutions need to be sought. However, they do not in themselves reveal the forces that might energize change. This book will examine proposals that are made for a way out of social degeneration. These include economic revival and growth, rational analysis and planning, holistic awareness and creativity, and, ultimately and inevitably, spiritual insight and values. At a later stage it will be suggested that purely secular solutions are inadequate, but before that stage is reached it is necessary to be clearer about the significance of the distinction between the secular and the spiritual.

Breaking the spiritual taboo

Simply stated, and later chapters will develop the idea, the contention here is that our hope of locating a unifying purpose to life, one that will allow us to become regenerative in education and society, depends upon the recognition that we are all spiritual beings. No human being is without the essential quality that grants admission to the non-material world. This truth of experience can be stated at several levels. Our minds, though apparently connected to our brains, cannot be linked any closer than by a parallel line with the physical experience of the body. The mind seems to hover above the body. The level at which other people engage our feelings of love, sympathy, loyalty, or simply the conviction of shared experience, suggests another kind of exposure to the non-material. The idea of a divine presence that brings hope, security and peace, is for many the most vital assurance of the spiritual dimension to life. This does not imply that the notion of the spiritual can only be used with reference to God, but simply that awareness of the divine represents the ultimate spiritual experience. The unifying factor may not in practice be an explicit religious belief, but the acceptance of such an ultimate power over human existence is clearly unifying not just in awareness or belief, but in meaning, purpose and direction for life.

The search for a starting-point which is a source for values in life as well as in education, need not be, and I would even say should not be, a matter for debate. Some argue that truth emerges from conflict, but I think this is true only for a very limited kind of truth. Truth for living comes out of openness to others, experience of sharing and of loving, and an acceptance of what we are. The implications of this conviction for my present task are that I shall find truth, and of course error, that is light and shadow, in almost every direction I look. I must indicate what I regard as error, but this is in passing in order to arrive at what is more true for me. In this sense, even what I see as another's error may become a contribution to my truth, and I can be grateful for their view, even while my reason or my experience may not be able to associate it directly with a unifying purpose for life.

What is being proposed here is an attitude not simply of critical openness, which is indispensable, but of conviction that we do actually know ways forward. We have forgotten so much that we have known as a civilization. Thus, the main task is not to predict and imagine things that have never been thought of before, so much as standing still, keeping our peace, and considering what manner of being we are. Our conclusions can be radical. In fact they need to be. One radical conclusion to be drawn, I suggest in this book, is that the taboo that modern society has imposed upon the spiritual vision of humanity issuing from a Creator's intention must be broken. In other words, enquiry into questions of ultimate meaning and purpose must again be seen as a meaningful activity in itself. I do not believe that there is a way forward in the contemporary cultural crisis without acknowledging this. Lacking meaning and purpose condemns so many initiatives to run into the sand, and, whatever convictions some independently-minded individuals may have, much of western society and education can be said today to be lacking a fundamental sense of meaning and purpose, despite the camouflage of materialistic pragmatism.

If we could succeed in breaking the taboo on the spiritual that constrains our societies and their educational systems, forcing learning into a soulless, utilitarian mode, we might release deep inspirations of creativity, imagination, care, service and happiness that our civilization seems in danger of losing. We see pale shadows of such renewal in education in the commitment of professional teachers, the integrity of their teaching, the excitement of learners at certain stages of their schooling, the atmosphere of some schools in which the staff work as a united team. The same ideal can also be glimpsed from its shadow side in the cynicism and demoralization of many teachers and the restlessness and resentment of the young, for such attitudes are the expression of disappointment at the absence of what might have been.

Inevitably, we enter the discussion of the spiritual in the recognition that there is a great diversity of meanings attached to the term. Indeed, it could be useful simply to catalogue its varying interpretations. But, however valuable this might be as an intellectual exercise, it would be meaningless for present purposes. I propose instead to argue and in part affirm the perspective to which I have myself come, and which I believe offers common ground for others, despite the strange mixture of fascination and aversion that is evident when the topic arises. If there is a taboo on the spiritual in everyday discussion, this must be because many feel their rights as fully developed human beings are abridged by invoking a spiritual dimension, and especially a spiritual power. In the minds of some it adds nothing, and it threatens to take away. It refers back to a fog of mediaeval mysticism, of religious oppression, in short, of ignorance; and it is therefore treated with profound suspicion (Hay, 1985).

The very fact that this subject is so difficult to address, that it arouses feelings of antagonism, threat or jealousy about the philosophical or religious terms in which the problem is posed, is in itself evidence that there is a raw nerve. My hope is that by seeking to expose this nerve, to deal with it with as much integrity, straightforwardness and conviction as I can, I may be able to provide stimulus and encouragement to others who are searching for an alternative vision for society and for education. Only a strongly self-critical, even self-denying process of reflection on the subject can be regarded as appropriate. Each contributor to the enquiry needs to become a source of vision and empathy. We can attain this awareness only by growing humanly and spiritually. It is not a question of brainpower. Sheer intelligence only makes things more and more complex, whereas we need to make them more and more simple. For example, taking the possibility that everything takes its 'true' value and meaning from a Creator, how likely is it that human intelligence will ever discover this? Instead new meanings will be invented, developed, imposed and defended. Spiritual awareness involves taking down such mental fortifications, clearing out the accumulated stock of ideas and interpretations of experience. It is not that we are worthless, but that we have been too obsessed by our worth in materialist terms

Materialist and spiritual viewpoints have been held in tension for centuries, and yet it seemed that within our own lifetimes the tension had slackened. God was dead. Only human reason remained to save us from the forces of degeneration, illness, war, poverty and ignorance. Science, technology and politics have been applied to these tasks perseveringly in recent decades without any real sense of confidence about managing the future. What can be seen, though, is that the self-affirmative streak in our culture has grown powerfully, that interests, rights, freedoms, individuality, have been ever more forcefully explored. No one could any longer argue coherently against such values, which comprise the conventional wisdom of our day, but they are in a vacuum. There is no sense of what they are ultimately for, other than self-enhancement; and humanity loses its vision.

The implication is that we should be searching for alternatives to pragmatic and rationalist solutions to educational problems of the present day. But any alternative is going to be costly. The price will not be high in financial terms. Quite the contrary, for there will need to be a different attitude to money as our way of counting costs. The price to be paid will lie in the limits that will need to be imposed on individual expansion. A similar argument is put forward by world-renowned economists and statesmen in the notion of 'limits to growth'; but this is a solution from the 'head' (Independent Commission on International Development Issues, 1980). It does not tackle the personal level, of 'heart' and 'guts', where we are motivated by love, care, fear, greed, anger, jealousy and pride. Before there can be change in these respects a holistic or spiritual vision is necessary. The price would have to be borne by everyone, even though, paradoxically, if all were willing to pay it all would gain. We can measure this price only by reviewing where we stand in our dominant values, experience and beliefs. The value questions have got to be asked. If we begin collectively to change our source of conviction and, let us say, live more from the heart, and less from the head or the guts, then that may be the point of transition to a more widely shared awareness of the spiritual.

Map of the values terrain

The final task of this initial chapter is to suggest a way of mapping the values that are being or could be adopted as a basis for educational policy-making and practice. The range of choice needs to be articulated, if only to make it clear that there is a choice, that all educational viewpoints involve assumptions and influences that can be accepted or denied. Three main values perspectives are identified: the rationalist, the holistic and the spiritual. Although these can be analytically separated, and do in practice exist in exclusive forms (categories A, B and C in Figure 1), there is a variety of overlaps, linkages and syntheses that can also be distinguished (categories D to G). The model is not in any sense explanatory; it merely provides a convenient and no doubt provisional

17

organizing framework for the ensuing discussion, which outlines the main characteristics associated with each perspective, and identifies some of the key issues raised by them for educational policy and practice. These details are largely illustrative, since the main burden of the exposition of the values perspectives is deferred to Part two.

(A) Pragmatic values (rational)

The foremost value perspective in most western educational systems in the 1980s has developed from the rationalist ideology that perceives the market as the best mechanism for deciding choices and solutions, not just in the economy but throughout the public services as well. Monetarism and its endorsement of the market mechanism are offshoots of utilitarianism, a philosophy of the industrial era founded on the pragmatic ideal of the greatest happiness of the greatest number. Such philosophies are rationalist in the sense that they reflect theories of human behaviour based upon the assumption of an averaging out in favour of a best fit solution, whatever the actual decisions of individuals. Part of this rationality is the political calculus of individuals and groups concerned to maximize their own advantages. Thus, whatever the validity of the main assumptions being made by this school of thought, it does necessarily encourage the growth and flourishing of a variety of interest groups. The functioning of such groups leads to inequalities of status and power which are accepted as inevitable concomitants of a free, or unregulated market.

The issue that presents itself most forcefully in examining pragmatic values is the extent to which the fate of less participant groups and individuals represents an acceptable price to pay for the market system to operate, and what importance is attached to this aspect. We would expect that the market ideology would most appeal to those who were prepared powerfully to espouse sexist or racist positions, those who represented transnationals or the interests of the industrialized societies, or those who used the media and the materialist expectations of people to pacify and to neutralize public opinion and weaker opposition groups at home or abroad. It is inevitable that pragmatic values privilege those who already control resources and attach blame to those who fail to survive in the market. Rationally, the unemployed can be blamed for their condition. Whether or not it is fair to blame them is, however, a much more complex question that requires a close knowledge of the particular economic system. Another consequence of the market system is that those who fail gradually move more and more to the periphery, either into unemployment or as economically inactive people who no longer believe that participation in the economy, or even in the society, can bring them any benefits. This retreat by the weaker members of the society is accompanied by the advance of centralized economic

Figure 1 Map of the values terrain

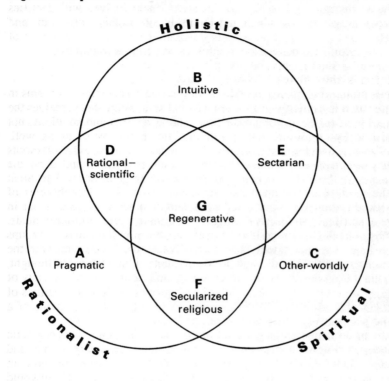

The three main perspectives	Exclusive forms
Rationalist values	**A** Pragmatic values
Holistic values	**B** Intuitive values
Spiritual values	**C** Other-worldly values

Areas of linkage and synthesis
D Rational – scientific values
E Sectarian values
F Secularized religious values
G Regenerative values

decision-making, not all of it by government, but all tending to secure the status quo and to favour decisions made in line with rational economic objectives, which may themselves be highly partisan in their effects.

A culture of possession reinforces material advantages, rewards enterprise and industry, builds upon success, maximizes the useful, and defends the 'haves'. These effects are equally visible in the non-monetary sphere of education, especially in Britain, where education is explicitly justified in terms of how well it can contribute to wealth-creation, useful production, and the development of talents desired by employers (DES, 1985a). The rationality of this system follows its own logic: it is not necessary to ask teachers or children what they want from education. If their needs are significant enough they will emerge in the market negotiation. No specialized machinery is needed. The question is how much such values and ways of thinking have to do with education as it is perceived by those with other ideologies, let alone in a spiritual perspective. Pragmatic thinking and politics tend to substitute the lesser gods of money, power and self-interest for the spiritual. To what extent, then, has education been co-opted to serve external political ends, and to satisfy particular group interests as distinct from the needs of learners using the system?

(B) Intuitive values (holistic)

The perspectives which will be referred to as holistic see the human as part of an ever-changing global or cosmic reality, and this entails an understanding of human beings as body, mind and feelings (Roszak, 1981; Bohm, 1981; Davies, 1984). According to this view, we all have needs and desires that go beyond rationality, and we have a subjective or intuitive awareness of our constantly evolving experience within a totality that cannot be grasped either by the mind or through the senses. This larger reality is sometimes termed spiritual, without necessarily invoking the existence of a deity. While there is no organized or consistent view, holistic philosophies tend to emphasize the ecological dimension, to favour such causes as peace and human rights, to endorse maximum variety in lifestyle and culture, and to trust experience and feelings more than abstract ideas, rational conclusions and scientific theories. Such a perspective can be extremely fertile in generating modes of human development, but how can it be brought to the service of formal educational practice? In its exclusive form, it necessarily lacks a detailed conceptual structure since it rejects the notion of reality as rationally defined. Should we not therefore look to this perspective for relevant values and insights for coping with specific learners, learning situations and activities rather than with organizational and curricular systems?

(C) Other-worldly values (spiritual)

The ambiguity of the term spiritual has already been discussed. If we retain it here to refer to what is distinct from the holistic, the point of the distinction can only be to introduce the sense of the divine. Uses of the term spiritual in any other sense will, for present purposes, be consigned to the category of the holistic. Other-worldly values represent the most exclusive category of the spiritual, where, for example, religious views belong to a privatized or subjective realm, and there is little or no concern to relate beliefs to everyday experience or to a broader social context. The most widely recognized instances have thus not developed to meet a new need but rather to preserve an old faith and practice. For example, ultra-orthodox Judaism involves turning from the rest of the world, and, leaving aside the related political manifestations of Zionism, any engagement with the wider society is largely in terms of the struggle to maintain valued religious observances against the pressures of secularization. Christian groupings vary in the degree to which they commit themselves to proselytizing activity in the wider society, but none the less consider themselves to have privileged access to divinely inspired truth.

The major faiths thus tend to have very forceful views of what is to be regarded as appropriate education, prescribing not just curricula but beliefs, values and behaviour as well. The characteristic of such approaches is the acceptance of both an inner self and beliefs in mysteries, such as of faith and eschatological hope, which are not amenable to rational analysis. Adherents thus reject philosophical relativism and are committed to a particular vision of reality. Is there a risk for society, for example in the socializing of the young, that, in the context of a lack of widespread reflection on the spiritual, the vacuum left will be neither criticized nor countered? Is there, in contrast, a spiritual vision of the world that will make a positive difference, even in social and political terms, and if so under what conditions? Or is the spiritual so closely tied to the priority of belief in another world that it can continue to be dismissed with impunity by earthly powers as a matter for free personal choice?

(D) Rational–scientific values (rational–holistic)

There is a variety of rationalist perspectives which offer philosophical and, within their terms of reference, comprehensive understandings of the nature and finality of humanity, society and education. To a degree such perspectives, which include the Marxist, the liberal–pluralist and the humanist, show holistic aspirations. They are quite distinct positions each of which claims the moral high ground for its rational–scientific understanding of reality. Marxism offers a total and definitive interpretation of human reality which is atheistic, materialist and dialectical, that is to say based upon the continually renewed struggle of economic and political interests which are mutually exclusive. The moral element comes from the Marxist identification with the worker as the critical contributor to production, and therefore the most deserving case. In contrast, the liberal–pluralist theories of reality are agnostic, individualistic in the final analysis, and tied for their moral legitimacy to notions of human rights and respect for social contracts. Third, the humanist perspective is a minority view, but an important one. It is also atheistic, seeing humanity as the apex of development, and looking to the self-perfecting of humanity, including the founding of morality, by the use of reason.

What these perspectives have in common is that they imply educational models that are rational, legal and constitutional. Policy solutions are presented as empirically founded, but tend to be more and more compulsorily applied, according to the degree of administrative centralization achieved. Although global in intent, such perspectives begin and end in the human mind. The reality that they encompass exists either in the mind or in the material universe. And yet relativism is the stuff of modern scholarship. So, in rationalist terms, the question has to be posed: where shall we stand to educate, when it is our very culture that appears to be failing us? Is there an alternative to the rational, and could our minds and our institutional arrangements for education ever accept it if there were?

(E) Sectarian values (holistic–spiritual)

Where there is an explicit commitment to the spiritual, holistic perspectives are apt to lead to a variety of dogmatic forms, such as sects or cults with a strong belief in their own truth, illumination or mission. Educational policies vary from the progressive liberal to the authoritarian, according to the strength of such commitments, but general characteristics of these groupings are a rigid membership boundary, internal hierarchies, and various levels of initiation. In educational terms, such associations are often extremely creative and effective, whether in proselytizing or in applying the energies of their adherents to secular tasks. It is not surprising that people can be swept away by the new synthetic teachings of cults combining, however incongruously, religion, psychology, even behavioural psychology, and big business. Is this kind of 'new truth' not even more threatening to secular society than those of an exclusively other-worldly character? Are we entering an era of heavy persuasion and indoctrination which could take us far beyond the often amateur emotionalism of the TV evangelists? And how will education provide or develop resources to counteract such manipulation?

(F) Secularized religious values (rational–spiritual)

There is one other variant of value perspectives which we will need to distinguish before considering a possible synthesis, and that is the accommodation made between rationalist and spiritual or religious viewpoints, to the extent of a virtual conflation of faith and reason. Since the spiritual is a taboo area for the rationalist and for the modern pragmatist, in that it is regarded as unacceptable to postulate a superior force to human reason, the formula of institutionalizing religion has provided an appropriate compromise. Established churches, often with bishops and other leaders nominated or approved by governments, religious practices adapted to civic ceremonials, theological arguments heavily informed by political priorities, moral codes assimilated to capitalist or socialist models, the relegating of religious theories to areas of science where there are still unsolved problems, thus creating a 'god of the gaps', are all common features of contemporary secular societies.

In educational policy-making such viewpoints can be powerful, as evidenced in Britain by the amendments to the Education Reform Bill which were obtained in the House of Lords in 1988 by leading Christian figures. But the concessions demanded are rarely radical. Harmonizing conscience with respectability, or even with fashion, is always a trap for churchmen. But is there now a risk of abandoning religious faith to rationality, or reasonableness? In what circumstances can there be genuine spiritual leadership from hierarchies and established figures in the institutional churches?

(G) Regenerative values (rational–holistic–spiritual)

The model that has been followed in these pages postulates three basic positions, the rationalist, the holistic and the spiritual, but also three intersecting positions, which have already been outlined, and finally a synthesis of all of these, which can now be suggested. A view of humanity which embraces mind, heart and spirit, requires a linking perspective, one which is not provided by any of the value positions so far advanced. Presumably it will not be difficult to agree on the need for the rational component, despite the fact that many believe rationalism to have been over-emphasized in contemporary culture and education. The holistic perspective has become less problematic in recent years, as one discipline after another searches for less rationalistic alternatives. Psychology, physics, biology, medicine, art, even economics, are all cases in point, as well as education itself.

The area where we can expect most difficulty in securing links is the spiritual. First of all, there is a problem of definition which has already been briefly mentioned. Even if we take the spiritual to imply the divine, as has been proposed here, what do we mean by the divine? We may think of a universal force, a power independent of humanity, a creator whose creatures we are, a source of existence outside space and time, a non-personal entity, or a personal God who knows us individually and has claims on us. The minimum accommodation to the spiritual would be to grant that we are not totally conditioned or determined by our physical experience and senses. If we go beyond this, it is to acknowledge that we know the spiritual as a greater force, that is, we can only know it by acknowledging our human limits. In fact, if we do not see that we are ultimately dependent on a greater power, we cannot recognize divine existence. If, on the other hand, we subordinate human reason to the divine, then it follows that our individual and collective wills, purposes and destinies are not the most important elements of reality. We will be looking for intimations of a greater value and purpose than we could ourselves conceive. Ultimate reality and truth may not be ours to know, but what if they are known by an infinite, all-knowing God?

Such a value synthesis, as represented by category G, has profound implications for education. If, for example, there was a widely and sincerely held belief that human beings were creatures of a loving God, destined to a spiritual existence beyond material existence, then the knowledge and service of that God would necessarily be included in any educational programme. The rational element of education would simply have to make space for a larger purpose. To return to the question raised at the beginning of this chapter, is this awkward intrusion of the spiritual simply a semantic matter, an attempt to inject a little dignified high-mindedness into the educational sphere which has been colonized by utilitarians, or is it the opening of a window to wider dialogue in the stuffy house of rationalism that can let in daylight and air to regenerate education?

What signs are there that the kind of value synthesis being suggested here, even a turning of the tide (Ward, 1986), could be taking place, and how seriously is this possibility going to be taken in the worlds of professional and lay public opinion? These are the issues towards which this work is pointed, towards which it will work its way along paths which, by definition, cannot be wholly rational. If the venture is to any extent successful it must challenge educational practice, bolster initiatives in experiential, holistic and spiritual learning and development, and possibly help to free creative forces which have been locked up because we do not know how to recognize or use them.

Part two

Alternative perspectives

Chapter two

The market economy of education

> In view of the benefits of education for the under-fives, and
> parental demand for its provision, the Government will make it its
> aim that its plans for LEAs' expenditure should allow provision
> attributable to under-fives to continue in real terms within broadly
> the same totals as today.
>
> (DES, 1985a: 40)

Far from regretting, as some educators do, that education cannot be
teased apart from politics, I see the whole relevance of this book as
depending upon education's potential to impact upon the political world
through its concern with values. The direction of influence in our times
has become so much the other way around that education is discussed as
if it should be at the service of the political world. This is a matter of the
greatest concern, because education is much more than politics, and the
kind of politicizing education has suffered has been the result of the
over-simplification rather than the refinement of public decision-
making. Education is brought to reflect the attitudes of the nation
through an impersonal process similar to the way the stock market
expresses its hopes and fears. Inevitably, then, schools and any other
educational institutions tend to exhibit the strengths and shortcomings
of the society that has, historically and politically, given them their
purpose and their shape.

Education in modern society has either been trivialized by becoming
a hobby for the affluent, or it has degenerated into being seen as
providing a meal-ticket for the less privileged. The 1960s-style options-
based curriculum, in which any whim might be satisfied, discouraged
the kind of thoughtfulness that concerned itself with fundamental
values. It was this very anarchy which, while it seemed like a freedom,
has set off such a strong reaction. Throughout the formerly liberal democracies education is now being required to give a public account of itself
as either an item of consumption for which an economic cost has to be
paid, or an investment from which an economic return can be derived.

To chart the course of public policy in education into the late 1980s would be a massive, and no doubt enlightening task, but this is far from my purposes here. My basic concern is that education is increasingly being treated as if it were simply a commodity in a market economy, and that because of this the human person is displaced, their rights, needs and wants disregarded, except in so far as these can generate a monetary transaction. It is not difficult to see justification for the policies that have evolved in many western societies which have introduced a strengthening of good housekeeping into education. Thrift has its place in any rationally ordered society, where resources are scarce, or at least limited, and where the balance between social rights and duties needs to be consciously maintained across a vast complex of social, economic and political relationships. However, it is where this rationale abruptly ends, and what it does not include, that is of primary interest here and corresponds to category A values as represented in Figure 1. This chapter, therefore, does not seek to encompass the undoubted vitality of much contemporary educational innovation, but reviews the market economy of education as succinctly as possible, as only a stage on the way to broader and philosophically more comprehensive alternative perspectives. The discussion centres upon educational policies in England, not because this is the only relevant example but because it is a particularly clear one. References to other societies are included, and could easily be extended.

Political and educational pragmatism

The dominant form of thinking in education in western societies today might be termed pragmatic or proto-rationalist for, while it does exhibit a certain logic in the way it orders reality in terms of preferred ends, these are largely short-term in perspective and fragmentary in scope. There is little evidence of developed philosophical or moral thinking behind current official educational proposals in Britain. Statements of educational aims are either brief and general in character, or they are entirely omitted, as in the case of the paper issued by the Department of Education and Science to introduce its 1987 proposals for a national curriculum policy (DES, 1987). The source of this kind of thinking in current British policy-making is monetarist economics, a highly instrumentalist view of the world, deriving its values from the creation and possession of wealth rather than from any universal good. Inevitably, since wealth is finite, but the desire for it not so, any values deriving from it tend to divide people's interests and perspectives. The larger question which will need to be addressed throughout this book is whether the notions of interest and value are as interchangeable as they are sometimes assumed to be.

Economic and social arguments

In Britain, this kind of thinking, which is far more widely accepted than merely by the Government, has been especially in evidence since the mid-1970s oil price crisis and the massive rise in unemployment which followed it. It showed up in education in the Callaghan Ruskin College speech in 1976, in which the then- Prime Minister, James Callaghan, reflected upon the role to be played by various educational reforms in meeting new social and economic needs. With the benefit of hindsight, the speech now reads as a wise and politically skilful one, which resulted in a major reforming programme without alienating the professionals. Among its most interesting arguments on a present day reading are those for the desirability of a national curriculum, and for the need for education and industry to come closer together so that schools could hear the complaints of industry, particularly about the standards of numeracy of school leavers, and thus more easily meet industry's educational requirements. Callaghan was careful to question whether industry's own shortcomings could account for criticisms about basic skills and attitudes, and he made a point of the need to balance educational aims between personal development and fitting people for a job of work.

> The goals of our education, from nursery school through to adult education, are clear enough. They are to equip children to the best of their ability for a lively, constructive place in society and also to fit them to do a job of work. Not one or the other, but both.
>
> (Callaghan, 1976)

These themes have gathered enormous momentum since, especially with the development of the Manpower Services Commission (previously known as the MSC, but which has since evolved into the Training Agency) as a powerful force in the control of the development of education and training. The Conservative Government which came to power in 1979 continued and radicalized this emergent pragmatism as a conscious policy, and built on a monetarist basis a range of sectoral policies, including policies for education, training and employment which were now seen primarily as a nexus of programmes responding to essentially economic priorities.

Matching this economic re-structuring was a similar *laissez-faire* evolution of social policy. By the mid-1980s, official Britain had rejected the notion of a welfare state and the attitudes of solidarity and compassion that went with it. The very idea of compassion attracted the political epithet 'wet', with its overtones of immature romanticism. Within such a context, opposition to sexism, racism, nationalism, and the over-valuing of the northern hemisphere in the same way that sexism and racism over-value one particular sex or race, became becalmed. The 1980s saw a resurgence throughout the western industrialized world of more aggressive social policies that gave no quarter to the weak, the minorities or the unemployed. It was decades since it had appeared so legitimate to blame the victims of social and economic disadvantage.

Policy-making came to be set in a framework of values that, however rational they might be in their own terms, are socially divisive in the way in which they marginalize the politically weaker sectors of society. The contemporary 'yuppie' syndrome is one of the manifestations of such values – but others are sexism, economic and cultural nationalism, privatization, and various forms of elitism that amount to a crude form of self-reliance that does away with trusting, negotiating and cooperating with others. These values, allowing that they can be called values, in that they represent an existential option rather than merely an economic policy – provide the security of working only with the known, and eliminate the threat of having to recognize other people's views, of being disrupted, of having to change or give way, or of having to cope with being frustrated.

There was a considerable groundswell of support for this new pragmatism in education, not only in Britain but in the United States and Western Europe. It was widely claimed that schools were inefficient in teaching basic skills essential to economic survival. In Europe especially, academic education was strongly criticized, first by liberals and de-schoolers and then by the industrial world, both arguing in a surprisingly complementary way that the most 'accomplished' products of education were incompetent, that school was dead, and that the knowledge, skills and attitudes resulting from formal education needed to be extensively unlearnt and replaced.

The 'end of ideology' had been proclaimed in the US in the 1960s (Bell, 1960), at a time when it appeared that social and economic problems were finding their solutions. Industrial and military demands reflected key interests rather than refined theories of society, as a whole school of sociologists have shown in their researches. First Bowles and Gintis, and later Apple and others, plotted the development of the capitalist centralization of control over education. In *Schooling in Capitalist America*, Bowles and Gintis describe in their chapter 'The Long Shadow of Work' the way that the economy influences the educational system (Bowles and Gintis, 1976). Apple, writing at a later date, when educational cutbacks had begun to affect American society, reports that:

At both the local and federal levels, movements for account-ability, competency-based teacher education and testing, systems management, standardized text books, mandated 'basics', academic standards, and so on are clear and growing.

(Apple, 1986: 129)

Pressures by government to gain greater centralized control over the curriculum have become widespread in many western democracies, such as Australia and New Zealand, as well as Britain and the United States, but for pragmatic economic and political reasons rather than articulated ideological ends. In continental Europe similar forces have become active, not in the traditional form of rigid centralization of authority but through policies framed to manipulate attitudes and behaviour of the young to cope pragmatically with youth unemployment that was being experienced throughout the European Community.

Vocationalization of the curriculum

From 1976 onwards, the EEC was able to generate support from member states for a programme of educational innovation, known as the *Action Programme for Education from School to Working Life*. With its endorsement for active learning methods, out-of-school experience, links with industry, and the learning of useful knowledge, skills and attitudes, the Action Programme has run ever since and has gone far to create a common European approach in these matters. In its second phase (1983–87), the Action Programme gave priority to reinforcing links between schools and the business world. This meant the development of such features as work experience, and education for enterprise, for example through mini-companies, and in turn led to a final statement, with the title of *Transition Education for the 90s*, which made recommendations for action in the priority areas of: schools and the world of work, guidance, school failure, in-service training for teachers, drawing 'especially on all activities involving contact and cooperation with the outside world', gender equality 'in order to widen the range of subject and vocational choices for girls', and support by parents (European Community Action Programme, 1988: 59–64). This massive programme of curriculum innovation was based upon a whole-hearted acceptance of the wisdom of subordinating education to the market economy, and a notion of vocation as a response to the market rather than to a 'calling' from within. In this sense, educational pragmatism in Europe had reached an apotheosis (Plunkett, 1986a).

Similar programmes of vocational and professional education and training were developed in the United States, but the kinds of attacks upon general academic education which had been so common in England and France since the 1970s had had less impact in the United States. One area in which American experience has foreshadowed current developments in Britain is in the advent of testing intended to

31

improve the standards of schools, together with the phenomenon of teaching to the tests which has become widespread. This is also a worry in the minds of many British educationists. It has been found that there is a competency-testing programme for students in thirty-eight of the fifty states of the US (Apple, 1986: 147). A curriculum with an emphasis upon measurable outcomes can be seen to have been emerging over the past decade in Western Europe also, as doubts about the performance of schools grew.

In the Britain of the 1980s, a strong tide of official scepticism about education took the form of blaming the schools for a range of the nation's ills, including youth unemployment and misbehaviour, and the lack of innovatory attitudes and skills amongst managers and workers in commerce and industry. With subsequent economic recovery and growth, however, there were no apologies, no reversals of these criticisms – which confirms that they had an ideological rather than a purely empirical basis. It was essential to the new, market orientated view of society that education should no longer be allowed any independence from the economic system. The arguments were that education should pay its way as an investment, and that it would do this by making a greater contribution to wealth-creation in the community. This would be in part achieved by the encouragement in schools of activities and attitudes supportive of enterprise, and also by greater formal accountability by schools to society for their use of financial and human resources. Commenting on a series of Government and other public reports on education in the US, Apple reports a similar tendency to sweep awkward problems under the carpet by blaming the schools:

> One major response of the reports is to blame our economic problems on our educational system...thus a large part of the solution lies in making our schools and their curricula more responsive to industrial and technological needs.
>
> (Apple, 1986: 136)

Centralization of educational policy-making

The late 1970s in Britain saw a phase of unrelenting but largely uncoordinated activity in the education and training sectors, with the introduction by the MSC of the Youth Opportunities Programme, the Youth Training Scheme, and schemes for the training of the adult unemployed. In a separate programme of innovation, the Department of Education and Science promoted the City Technology Colleges, and criterion-based testing and examinations, which were proposed in a number of significant reports, of which the most relevant to our purposes here were *Better Schools* (DES, 1985a), *The School Curriculum from 5 to 16* (DES, 1985b) and *The National Curriculum*

5–16: a Consultation Document (DES, 1987). Together with the MSC, the DES introduced the Technical and Vocational Education Initiative (TVEI). This intensive educational programme was backed by substantial and specifically targeted financing in its pilot phase, and constituted an attempt to change education by central guidance in a direction consistent with the Government's economic priorities.

The publication of these educational proposals merely confirmed the strongly established trend towards pragmatic policy-making being followed in other sectors of government. This perspective was now showing itself as a strongly skewed selection of principles for government that reflected a short-term political calculus. Major priorities were being accorded to wealth-creation and a firmly nationalistic stance, while the distribution of wealth and of opportunities to acquire it were seen as depending strictly upon market place mechanisms. Although pragmatism has an honourable history in Britain, the line being taken by the Government in the later 1980s had shifted about as far as could be imagined from the still pragmatic democratic socialism of post-war Europe (Crosland, 1956; Myrdal, 1960). At the same time, the United States, which has in modern times accomplished centralization, or federalization of education through financial aid programmes, is moving towards strategies for controlling the work of teachers,

> ...so that it is linked more directly to specific behavioural outcomes and directed by managerial techniques and ideologies and bringing curricular goals and materials into line with the industrial, military and ideological 'needs' of a relatively small but powerful segment of the American public.
>
> (Apple, 1986:8)

Victorian values and the schools

A much featured aspect of the British Conservative Government of the early 1980s was the fascination of some of its leaders with Victorian values. Their political expression came through speeches that emphasized industriousness, competition, individual effort, and education for prosperity, with every benefit being assigned an economic value. Consequently, education was to be evaluated in terms of how well it served the economy, and how well it prepared its products for the labour market. Since the economy was altering fast mainly through the increasingly widespread applications of electronics, the schools were expected to run extra-fast to keep up. Education was encouraged with considerable financial inducement to adopt computers, to introduce liaison arrangements to help to foster cooperation with local industry, to emphasize work-related skill learning, to start business studies programmes, and to accept an ever greater accountability of both teachers and pupils through systems of assessment, profiling, appraisal and examinations. At the same time there was a noticeable slippage in curriculum priorities in the degree of concern for individual development, personal and social education, and the care of the socially disadvantaged in the inner cities, certainly as compared with educational policies of the 1960s.

The concept of the curriculum altered fast as a result of these new concerns. In the mid-1970s it could be encompassed by the eight areas of learning advocated by the Inspectorate, which represented an attempt to move rather gently away from a traditional subject-based curriculum; by a decade later, a ninth area, technology, had been added, and the areas were now of 'learning and experience' within what was called an 'entitlement curriculum' (DES, 1985b). No more than two years later attainment targets were proposed for a set of foundation subjects, which marked a noticeable drawing back from commitment to human development concerns. It is noteworthy that, although the paper introducing proposals for a national curriculum in 1987 cited as its aims 'preparation for adult life and work', it is only the concern for work that emerges clearly from the paper (DES, 1987). There is no hint of dissatisfaction with the schools' efforts to prepare for adult life more generally. This could not have been because the job was being done well, but could only reflect the fact that this was not seen as a priority concern by Government.

Even the values that might have been attached to social relationships in the curricula of education and training programmes, through such teaching areas as personal, social and moral education, community service, health education, or personal effectiveness, let alone matters of political controversy, were increasingly marginalized in successive curriculum documents. There was insufficient value consensus in official circles to support anything else. Thus, controversial issues were dealt with in terms of enquiry processes only; contentious substance was roundly condemned in such areas as peace studies. The official approach to Aids education is an interesting case: the opportunity to make a moral case was not taken, and the publicity hit a note of hysteria before settling down to put forward the facts in a rational but inevitably ineffectual information programme.

The only priority that was consistently maintained was the progressive vocationalization of the curriculum. Transition education programmes in schools were short term and negligent in their assumptions about young people, their needs, attitudes and potentials. While they may have succeeded in offering an opportunity to many who needed a positive role in the hiatus of leaving school without any clear occupational destination, such curricula suffered from too narrow a perspective in the light of current and foreseeable job opportunities. The net effect of the programmes was rather to ease recruitment and training problems for employers than to extend the educational principle of helping young people to fulfil their potential.

There is thus a subordination of learners to economic requirements. The curriculum is employer-led. Personal decision-making is to serve economic objectives and needs. Responsibility becomes less a personal ethic, and more a social obligation, but to the state and the economy rather than to the community. Growth in the economy and technological innovation become values in themselves. These factors force choosing, it is true, but in our societies they force specific choices. The moral element is virtually eliminated. The concern for the quality of life of young people who feel unsure, rejected, alienated and resentful, is absent.

Calling the schools to account

So strongly did the British Government embrace its market-based educational policy that education was lauded, in *Better Schools*, for outcomes which would never before have been seen as achievements. Results are looked for in quantifiable terms of standards reached, and this is taken to mean qualifications gained in public examinations. As the White Paper stated, '...for most pupils, the period of compulsory education culminates in assessment through public examinations' (DES, 1985a: 29). Content covered and skills acquired are assumed to be the critical outcomes, rather than learner satisfaction or fulfilment. Education was seen as an investment, which was nothing new. What was new, however, was that the economic return to investment in education was expected in the short-term. Education was to contribute to 'prosperity', as the introductory and concluding paragraphs of the document emphasized. This provides a rationale for resource allocation to specific areas of learning regarded as having the maximum relevance to economic opportunities. Thus, vocationally-orientated curricula are proposed at progressively earlier ages, and employers' requirements are taken as the most relevant criteria for guiding curriculum change.

Schools were to be held much more directly accountable to prominent social and economic interests. As a consequence, expenditures favouring disadvantaged groups, urban priority areas, which were not even mentioned in the 1985 report, or areas of education regarded as consumption, such as the aesthetic and artistic aspects of the curriculum, had a lower claim. Above all, personal and moral education received little attention, and a curriculum emerged that would give much greater emphasis to the training than to the development of young people. As an additional efficiency measure, differentiation of curricula would effectively separate academically inclined from other pupils, and those likely to be employed from those likely to be unemployed. Whatever the intention, particular sectional interests would be favoured. Solutions were to be imposed, by legislation and by administrative measures; choice would be confined in practice to those best equipped to know they can choose; and schools would be made to bear the blame for education's shortcomings, as if resources for learning and for staff development programmes for teachers could be treated as dispensable luxuries.

The National Curriculum

The logical outcome of this process for education in England and Wales came with the gradual emergence of a plan for a national curriculum. This had been in the mind of policy-makers from the late 1970s, as we have seen, and action was taken towards it in 1981 when LEAs were asked to communicate their curriculum guidelines to central government. The arguments for a greater degree of national influence over the curriculum were beginning to be accepted on all sides, but thinking generally seemed to be favouring a framework that would ensure that all pupils were treated equally, and those moving from one part of the country to another would not be disadvantaged. After the publication of *Better Schools*, Government notions of a national curriculum developed very swiftly. The 1987 legislative proposals saw the argument in broader terms, still within a market framework. A national curriculum would enable a better response to national needs; it would assist not only pupil mobility, but continuity of curriculum and progression of pupils between phases even where they do not move; above all, the existence of a national curriculum would permit a system of testing that would allow educational standards to be checked, maintained and, where necessary, raised.

These arguments undoubtedly counted on considerable political support, even though many professional educationists regarded them as simplistic and precipitate. In fact, new proposals were advanced so swiftly that there were awkward contradictions with established policies. Two examples are paramount for present purposes. The extension of the TVEI programme has been built around the notion of a curriculum core comprising several linked elements, including literacy and numeracy, personal effectiveness, information technology and work experience. The first indications about the National Curriculum omitted the personal and social development elements of the core, though it was later argued that this was not intended. There was a parallel situation in the case of religious education, which was an established part of the school curriculum that had barely been mentioned in the 1987 consultation document.

Both social and personal development and RE were at first downgraded by the National Curriculum proposals, and their relationship to the proposed foundation curriculum was uncertain. Here again, it was argued that the intention was not to bring about any change, and amendment was made to the Bill to ensure the continued protection of RE (Education Reform Act, 1988). However, despite a variety of disclaimers, and the acceptance of substantial amendments to the Bill regarding RE, the fundamental intentions of policy-makers remain in doubt in both these areas, which are exactly those which most tend towards an alternative curriculum. Subsequent policy decisions on financing of in-service training have provided the first clue that Government intentions are to limit severely the possibility of either of these two areas playing a major part in the National Curriculum. Of a total of £214m additional funds allocated to teacher in-service training for 1988–89, £1.1 was earmarked for religious education (*The Times*, 16 August 1988).

The reversion, in the rigid form of legislation, to a curriculum formed from single teaching subjects building upon required skill levels means that learners will face added difficulty in seeking any overall meaning and coherence in the curriculum, and this is a far cry from the programme that had for some years been nurtured with fervent Government backing through MSC school-based and post-school education and training programmes. No reasoned justification was offered for this change, though it is apparent that the voting public understand subjects like English and geography better than notions of personal effectiveness or personal, social, health and moral education.

The consultation document on the National Curriculum gave short shrift to 'personal qualities' because 'they cannot be written into a programme of studies or attainment targets'. But this was to accept that if something cannot be measured it cannot be discussed. It was however conceded that the foundation subject working groups, responsible for producing syllabuses, attainment targets and testing proposals, should have in mind such values as: 'self-reliance, self-discipline, an enterprising approach and the ability to solve practical real-world problems' (DES, 1987: 25). This is a narrow diet of values indeed, and still betrays the obsession with the market product. There is no philosophical enquiry and no concern with motivational issues, as if the nature of the 'real world', presumably of commerce and industry, were a matter of general consensus. The implication is that in the real world individuality is suspect, conformity is rewarded, and morals are guided by enterprise. The kind of learning that is called for cannot justifiably be called either educational or developmental.

An enterprise culture

In fact, in several ways the late-1980s version of educational pragmatism in Britain was a remarkably metamorphosed conservatism, less concerned with deep philosophical principles than with building a new 'enterprise' culture, rewarding the industrious and ensuring the effective selection of talent, the prosperity of the economy, and successful competition with other countries. Not only were there no misgivings about challenging the education professions, but measures that threatened the survival of the system of LEA-controlled schools and of the comprehensive system were confidently introduced by the Education Reform Act, 1988. The role of the Government, paradoxically, was to hold the ring very firmly to allow market decisions to be made, to allow schools to opt out of LEA control, to permit privatized, or 'independent-state schools' to emerge, to enable parents to expand and contract schools by their custom, and to let drop all educational innovations and developments which had not secured themselves a buying public. Significantly, the notions of 'clients' and 'customers' of education are scattered through the text of *Better Schools* (DES, 1985a).

This enterprise culture is associated in political rhetoric with opportunity and prosperity, but on any academic assessment it must rate as narrow, lacking in social or political vision, negative and blaming in its view of the place of education in the national culture, and stigmatizing in its implications for all those who lack enterpreneurial attitudes or capacities. In social and educational terms, such policies are divisive, and are certain to create greater marginalization of minorities in the community. No 'national' response was contained in the 1988 legislation to questions about the needs of pre-school children in difficult circumstances, the guidance of the academically or vocationally less well endowed, the socially disadvantaged, the culturally and environmentally demotivated, or even late developers.

The issue that arises is whether such pragmatic thinking is to be defended, as part of the rational adjustment of policies to circumstances, or whether the creation of a market economy of education is evidence of moral collapse. If the latter view were valid, then the current obsession with enterprise can be seen as part of a range of deviations from the line of civilization and betterment that humanity might have hoped would emerge from modern science, democratic society and more informed public opinion. In other words, how different is the market economy of education from the various forms of populist and demagogic thinking, such as is represented by the stereotyping values of sexism, racism, left and right extremism, and consumerism, which seem to persist in even the most sophisticated societies? Would it be surprising, indeed, if a society capable of harbouring stereotypes of materialist and other sectional interests, or which was merely a prey to such false values as the sexual liberty of the tabloids or the anti-values of cynical and satirical TV humour, should also produce an amoral and increasingly dehumanized educational system? This judgement has to be understood in the light of the neglect in recent official policy statements of discussion of the needs, wants or rights of children in the educational system, or of any serious acknowledgement of non-monetary values in education.

Another gap in pragmatic thinking about education is in the neglect of the needs of teachers and student-teachers. So long as teachers are seen as agents for a Government programme rather than professionals seeking to make their contribution according to their insights, skills and resources, their training will naturally be seen in the narrowest of terms. However, it is surely obvious that teachers cannot all be tarred with the brush of incompetence, irrelevance or idleness, and that they will need not only to cope with a whole battery of Government-sponsored innovations, such as the range of new testing duties required of the classroom teacher and the management tasks to be assigned to senior teachers, but also a more open-ended opportunity to come to terms with the new structure of the curriculum and especially the teaching of cross-curricular themes on which the broader education of their students will depend. The danger is that funds available for teacher in-service training will go only to the officially favoured innovations and that the further professional development of teachers will be forgotten.

The value of pragmatic values

An enterprise culture cannot be condemned outright, because it represents a rational attempt to order resources and to organize society in a situation of uncertainty and concern. It can be argued even on rational grounds, however, that it is an exaggerated and unbalanced response, that it leaves too much that is important out of consideration and prepares worse problems for the future. Beyond this, too, it can be affirmed rather than argued that the spiritual cost of an enterprise culture is very great, because it so successfully blocks all alternatives, and especially those that start from values of compassion, trust, sharing and love, rather than usefulness, possession, monetary value and self-interest.

It may be enlightening to ask to what extent have pragmatic values given an adequate response to the five propositions discussed in Chapter one. For example, when a Government document comments on its purpose to ensure a curriculum equipping all pupils with the knowledge, skills and understanding that they need for adult life and employment, and refers to 'the value that the school has added', as if to an item of manufacture, the atmosphere created is authoritarian (DES, 1985a: 4). If such values can command a political majority (Proposition 2) they are likely to be imposed both administratively and pedagogically. At this point the notion of values gives way to propaganda, because the benefits being promised are illusory for some of those being addressed. This is a case of values being used pragmatically rather than ethically.

In educational terms (Proposition 3), the assertion of central control by legislation and financial manipulation, as well as by the techniques of blaming teachers and condemning professional judgements made about the curriculum, which appear to be common developments throughout western society, are increasingly indoctrinatory. The notion of a fruitful dialogue between points of view is in danger of being discarded. Educational systems are being run to overly-technical criteria, and in ways that are antithetical to educational as opposed to economic thinking. The 'technical smörgasbord of the current school system, with its utter inability to distinguish between important and unimportant in any way other than the demands of the market' (Bloom, 1988: 59) is characteristic of other societies than just the American.

Market values cannot be the whole story in education, and it is sobering to reflect that the major priorities of the European Community in education and youth policy have to do with trimming education to industrial requirements so as to better prepare young people for adult and working life. The omissions from this programme are far more significant than its massive and successful innovation and development. At a recent dissemination conference aimed at examining the outcomes of the Community Action Programme, and entitled 'Schools and Industry: Partners for Education', the themes studied were:

> integration of link activities into the curriculum and guidance; adaptation of the curriculum to regional economic developments; education for enterprise; improving work experience schemes; provision of in-service teacher training; and the policy and practical support needed for regional and local school–industry linking bodies.
>
> (Eurydice Info, no.5, 1988)

There might be nothing to comment on adversely if other major conferences were looking at alternatives to 'industrialized' education, but such does not appear to be the case.

Far from enhancing the role and professional self-image of teachers, it might seem that educational reforms (Proposition 4) in many western contexts are deliberately constructed to marginalize and de-professionalize teachers, either by enforcing curricula that are designed to be teacher-proof, or by controlling teachers' work through testing and appraisal systems. The provisions of the Education Reform Act, 1988, in Britain, refer to teacher education only in relation to testing the National Curriculum. Given the widespread criticisms of teachers that have come from official sources over a period of years it is surprising that attention is not being given to reasons why teachers are not teaching satisfactorily, if that is the case, or why learners are not learning satisfactorily.

It seems obvious that many teachers have been deeply affected in their professional attitudes and values by being forced to maintain a confrontational stance. They feel demeaned by it, and they know that it is doing no good to their schools, to the atmosphere that they have known in the past, and which enabled them to speak to their pupils in terms of optimism and idealism about life. Teachers have grown ferociously defensive, and there is a mood of embitteredness which few have known before, and none as a general feature of life in schools. Because of the development of centralized financial and other controls, teachers' curriculum development activities no longer reflect their professional convictions so much as the prioritized in-service funding, secondment policies, arrangements for covering absences, special financing, and so forth. The result is that the curriculum is taking the shape intended by the policy-makers, but without carrying the conviction of the teachers along with it. There is a mood of resentment in the staffrooms which bodes ill for the system in the longer term. In fact, that is the crux of the matter. The conception of policy from the centre has been immediate, short-term, directed to specific ends. The lack of sympathy for longer-term objectives has meant that those who entered teaching with a motive of service to society are now severely disillusioned.

The acid test of the 'value' of pragmatic values lies in the extent to which the market economy of education is able to respect and involve people, and to enhance the quality of their lives. The criteria for judgement of this are of course problematic, but it has been argued that an essential one would be the furthering of self-determination or freedom for individual human beings (Proposition 5). Certainly Victorian values are of little help: as the obligation to work came to be seen more and more as a burden imposed by a powerful social and political system, as occurred particularly during the industrial revolution, the scope for choice was fundamentally restricted, however diversified the actual processes of the economy became. In fact, for many, there was no choice, as they had to do the work that their community did to fit into the economic system: agriculture, milling, manufacturing, and so forth. This image of work as enslaving has been handed down to us, and thus many have come to see work as an alienated part of their lives, the part they do not control, the part mortgaged to the economic system.

The forces that conspire to keep this image of work intact, such as the pressures of modern wealth-creation, competition, the career rat race, fears of redundancy and unemployment, the 'diploma disease', and the oppressiveness characteristic of many employers and financial bureaucrats, are all magnified by the corporate structure of modern economies and by the philosophy of governments which give rewards and honours precisely to those who have been most willing to accept the market discipline. One of the most outspoken critics of market philosophy in Britain has been the report on *Faith in the City*, where it is seen as responsible for a progressive division of rich and poor, and as 'a more or less crude exaltation of the alleged benign social consequences of individualized self-interest and competition' (Archbishop of Canterbury's Commission, 1985: 25). And what is true of the economic system is also true of the educational system. Education has always played the role of handmaid to the economy, even in the Middle Ages when it trained clerics and officials rather than primary-sector workers. Increasingly, with industrialization, education was compelled to justify itself by the employment to which it led. Nowadays, this has become axiomatic. We would not have the educational systems we do, were it not for the services rendered by education to the economy.

One of the characteristics of official educational policies in recent years in the United States, Britain and Europe has been to treat youth as a *problem*. This is the opposite of respect for persons. Young people are blamed for unemployment as if the possession of more examination passes would guarantee them jobs in modern economic conditions. It has not been honestly admitted that most of the special measures to train unemployed youth could at best alter the order in the queue for jobs, and young people cannot be blamed if they have realized this. Nor can young people be blamed for attitudes that appear selfish and morally indifferent if that is all they see around them. Propositions 1 and 5 are closely linked, in that a climate of rejection of young people as virtually redundant to society's needs, such as existed in the early 1980s, was likely to produce just the football hooliganism which so horrifies established society.

Furthermore, if education, as Proposition 3 implies, has also forsaken its vocation of seeking truth and enhancing the person, if it has become utilitarian and materialistic, so that there is no place for reflection, judicious criticism, warnings of dangers, or personal commitment by professionals, then no alternatives are being offered to the young. Added urgency is given to this matter by the fact that the 1990s are going to witness a huge reduction in numbers of school leavers coming onto the job market, so that it is clear that general education to help young people identify and test all their talents and to develop their judgement about their own values, lifestyles and other life decisions, including work, would be a preferable policy to current pragmatism, even on rational grounds.

It is of course essential that education should prepare young people for adult life and work, through appropriate curricula and teaching approaches, direct relationships between the educational system and the industrial world, and other such innovations. The limitation of a too highly focussed approach is that schools can end up seeking to give their students the meaning that their lives should have, rather than helping them to discover or decide about this for themselves. Fundamental decisions and understandings concerning the meaning and purpose of our lives cannot be pre-empted by authority, science, technology, pedagogy, and least of all by market mechanisms. Such philosophical and ultimately spiritual concerns are seriously threatened by the current priority given to material and worldly values. The pragmatic is the very antithesis of the spiritual.

The case being made against the market economy of education is a severe one, but that is because the issue is critical for the survival of human and spiritual values in modern society, and there is little indication that anything other than a revolution in values will suffice to alter current policy priorities. When the useful is preferred to the good, the measurable to the unique, the marketable to the fulfilling, and the technological to the moral and spiritual, as clearly appears in current policy statements concerning education, it is time to protest, and to look for another way of ordering matters. If education is rightly considered as too important to be left to the teachers, it is very much too important to be left to market mechanisms.

Chapter three

The education of the mind

The crisis of liberal education is a reflection of a crisis at the peaks
of learning, an incoherence and incompatibility among the first
principles with which we interpret the world, an intellectual crisis
of the greatest magnitude, which constitutes the crisis of our
civilization. But perhaps it would be true to say that the crisis
consists not so much in this incoherence but in our incapacity to
discuss or even recognize it. Liberal education flourished when it
prepared the way for the discussion of a unified view of nature and
man's place in it, which the best minds debated on the highest
level. It decayed when what lay beyond it were only specialisms,
the premises of which do not lead to any such vision. The highest
is the partial intellect; there is no synopsis.

(Bloom, 1988: 346–7)

It is of the nature of the human mind actively to seek understanding of
itself and of the world, and then to test and prove the validity of its
discoveries. This, it appears, is a never-ending task, yet one that never
causes discouragement. Just as we breathe from the day we are born
until the day we die, so we are always and inexorably faced with the
question of what is real for us, and what we should think and do about
it. The previous chapter considered one style of thinking, the pragmatic,
which emphasized immediate goals and results. But not all thinking is
of this kind. Even in our individual awareness, we feel engaged in a
continuous search for information or ideas that can be relied upon to
give a framework for our lives. On the one hand, we are pragmatic in
that we believe that we can store our knowledge from one day to guide
us the next, even if as a result we disconfirm something we previously
regarded as known, but on the other hand we commonly speak of
becoming older and wiser, as if sensing that with passing time and
accumulated experience we are enriched and more complete as persons.

The operative question that leads us on appears to be: what or where
is truth? We may never actually possess it to a degree that satisfies us,

but increasing our awareness of where we stand must be better than ignoring the assumptions of truth and falsehood that we currently hold, for we certainly do all hold some. If this is in principle valid for each of us individually, then it is not surprising that collectively the human race has searched persistently over the millenia of recorded history to extend its understanding of what could be regarded as real and true. The cosmologies of the Egyptians, the Torah of the Hebrews, the love of wisdom of the Greeks, the legal and administrative systems of the Romans, the theology of the Christians, the rationalism of the Cartesians and the Philosophes, the scientific enquiry of the German universities in the nineteenth century, and the linguistic analyses of the logical positivists in our own century, are all examples of the absorbing fascination with which the human mind seeks always to extend the scope of its awareness of what can be taken to be true.

The purpose of this chapter is to contrast with pragmatic thinking the more systematic, theoretical approaches by which we have sought to understand the world and society in order to be able to control and direct its development. Education has long been a major theme of such thinking, as a powerful means by which every aspect of life could be brought under the sway of rationally ordered rules and laws. The last two centuries have provided a history of such efforts, and the present task can only be to characterize them in general terms, so that the strengths and limitations of the kind of thinking associated with scientific rationalist values (category D in Figure 1) can be appreciated, and thus a clearer understanding gained of alternative, or at least complementary approaches.

Modern western education stems above all from a religious tradition which closely associated the individual, the Church and the state. The 'divine right' theory underlying the exercise of imperial and papal powers in mediaeval Europe left little room for dissent, and thus prepared the way for the mighty clashes that occurred first with the Reformation, then with the Enlightenment, and subsequently with Marxism. These rival and progressively articulated theories of society had implications for education that were distinctive in that they placed reliance upon critical reasoning rather than upon obedience to established authority assumed to have divine inspiration. Such thinking brought about major developments in historical terms, but the more immediate point to be made here is that the systematic rational thought which emerged from that history, whether applied to society or to education, takes us much further in its vision than can pragmatists in their insulated world.

Reason and rationalism

It is important not to confuse the human power to reason and what has historically come to be called rationalism. Reasoning opens up to us unlimited vistas of conceptualization, enquiry and recognition of relevant logical connections. In its most general sense, reasoning is the capacity of human beings to check data and pragmatic or intuitive thinking at each step of their way. Someone arriving at a railway station thinks to study the departures board and platform signs before jumping on a train, where otherwise habit, hunch and distraction might have dictated actions with potentially unfortunate results. Reasoning is a characteristically human activity, open-ended and undogmatic, and it is not without significance that the cognate word 'reasonable' has acquired a moral connotation, though a very limited one as will be discussed later.

Rationalism, with its characteristically modern variant, rational–scientific thinking, on the other hand, forms a particular type of systematic reasoning that encloses a peculiar paradox. It both proceeds on the implicit assumption that human thought can effectively deal with problems in such a way as to find solutions, and at the same time it depends upon the sceptical approach that is obliged to question all received knowledge, and all thinking which does not fit the rationalist model of explanation by reference to antecedent causes. The price to be paid is a high one. To illustrate the point, in his collection of essays entitled *The Art of the Soluble*, Medawar embarks upon a review of the work of Teilhard de Chardin, in which he brings to bear all his rational scepticism as a biologist. He castigates Teilhard for his looseness of expression, his philosophical and religious assumptions, his teleological preoccupations, and in the most intemperate language he dismisses him as a charlatan:

> The Predicament of Man is all the rage now that people have sufficient leisure and are sufficiently well fed to contemplate it .... Teilhard not only diagnoses in everyone the fashionable disease but propounds a remedy for it – yet a remedy so obscure and so remote from the possibility of application that it is not likely to deprive any practitioner of a living.
>
> (Medawar, 1969: 91)

Caught up in his intellectual system, Medawar appears unable to recognize his own emotions and fears. There is no foundation of values, or purposes, or even belief in the possibility of purposes other than those implicit in the intellectual system of rational–scientific enquiry.

It is not relevant here to appraise Medawar's essay as an exercise in rational–scientific criticism, but what it makes clear to me is that such rationality is a closed system. The limitations of such thinking have been indicated by Kuhn, in his work *The Structure of Scientific Revolutions* (Kuhn, 1970). Rational–scientific thinking rests upon a paradigm of enquiry which is itself replete with assumptions. The classic example of what Kuhn called a 'paradigm-shift', in which such assumptions suddenly crumble, was the Copernican revolution in astronomy. A similar scientific revolution can be said to have occurred when Darwin's theory of evolution through natural selection seemed to challenge the status of human beings as the central focus in the study of living forms. In a further paradigm-shift Pasteur revealed micro-organisms to be yet more basic common elements of life, and there was yet another when Einstein and other physicists virtually questioned the centrality of matter itself as the subject of scientific enquiry, both by demonstrating the validity of wave as well as particle theories of energy transmission, and by showing the determining nature of the influence of the scientific observer on the phenomena observed.

These paradigm-shifts constituted a succession of massively undermining assaults upon the established scientific thinking of their day. Thus, however rational it may be to seek always to be consistent in scientific thinking, through attention to both logic and sense-data, it is in fact not 'reasonable' to refuse to look at things in other ways. Medawar attacks indiscriminately precisely because his own paradigm is at risk when the radical possibility is raised that there may be a purpose to evolution, and a meaning to the universe. Newbigin, in his remarkably succinct exposition of the resistance to the gospel of what he calls the 'modern scientific culture' of the West, claims that it:

> ...has pursued the ideal of a completely impersonal knowledge of a world of so-called facts that are simply there, that cannot be doubted by rational minds, and that constitute the real world as contrasted with opinions, desires, hopes and fears of human beings, a world in which the words 'purpose' and 'value' have no meaning.
>
> (Newbigin, 1986: 148)

In these terms, therefore, the consideration of the spiritual dimension can be seen as representing another stage, a major paradigm-shift, in our understanding of ourselves and the world, as Chapter five will seek to illustrate.

Rational–scientific knowledge

A number of major philosophical problems that have arisen in the course of such human enquiries recur in reflections upon knowledge as it relates to education. The old question 'What knowledge is of most worth?' is thus never out of date. Is knowledge personal, or is it collective? That is, do we come to know in a unique way, or do we all possess knowledge in the same way and thus, potentially at least, all possess the same knowledge? This is the problem of the subjectivity or objectivity of knowledge. If we accept that knowledge is subjective, that an expression like 'white clouds' may be a merely verbal reality, because we cannot know if everyone using the expression means the same thing by it, then all that we purport to do collectively to influence, improve or control the world, for example through education, may simply be meaningless. If, on the other hand, things are not the case unless and until someone sees them to be so, or knows them to be so through sensory experience as the empiricist holds (Ward, 1986: 62), then the individual lives largely in a private world of meaningless fantasy, dependent entirely upon the plausibility structures of consensus and social control to be convinced of his very existence (Berger, 1980: 47–8). 'I think' is no longer sufficient reason for believing that 'I am'. But since most of us at least behave as if we accepted that there is knowledge that is subjective, the main philosophical problem we face is to discern where and how we can, with confidence, begin to deal with knowledge, and thus with reality, publicly rather than privately (Newbigin, 1986: 36).

In seeking to understand how we know what we know, philosophers of knowledge and of education have distinguished between purely rational, aprioristic thinking, and thinking which is empirical, or based upon sense-data. As a specific example of the former we might take the work of mathematicians who have elaborated an enormous fund of purely conceptual knowledge, though there is a much more general sense in which rational reflection on the educational process has contributed to thinking about the curriculum and organization of the educational system. Similarly, empirical enquiry has made its mark, especially through the introduction into educational curricula of experimental science which proceeds from hypotheses to the findings of laboratory tests. And the development of empirical educational research has contributed more generally to the actual organization of education, for example, through knowledge of more effective ways to group learners, to present materials or to ensure learning.

The other major consideration in thinking about the *real* is that rational design or random occurrence cannot suffice to account for why particular lines of thought occur at particular moments of history. Thought is also culturally located and formed. In other words, the priorities for enquiry, the information found to be significant, the shape taken by modes of thinking, and the connections made between ideas, depend upon sets of historical, geographical and sociological circumstances. This is not necessarily to say that reality itself is ultimately subjective, but that the attention paid to it at least is culturally relative. Some philosophers would go much further, and assimilate cultural relativism to the claimed subjectivity of knowledge. These two problems seem to me to be distinct, and thus I believe it is meaningful and likely to be profitable to conduct the present discussion of educational thinking within a particular cultural context, that of the western industrialized society, while recognizing that the discussion could legitimately have ranged much wider, and perhaps thus raised different issues of meaning and values.

Rational–scientific enquiry and education

We are used to characterizing the West as rational and technological, usually seeing this as a compliment to western development and civilization. We can, it is true, easily enough see benefits of this mode of thinking, enquiring and acting. Without it, there would simply be no modern world. Indeed, the rest of the world seems to cry out for western scientific knowledge, which is a form of wealth that the West has historically accumulated, largely through its formal educational institutions. Until recently it was almost a monopoly, but increasingly the West sees its status as challenged, at least technologically, and this could have the effect of reinforcing intellectualism and the dominance of rational forms of thinking, as a defence against economic defeats. At all events, we currently sense that the West passes judgement on the rest of the world from the lofty eminence of its intellectual pretensions, in science and technology, in politics, in culture, in education, in medicine, and even in religion, where nothing is taken seriously by western public opinion until it has been passed through the filter of rationalistic appraisal. The West has its paradigms of enquiry, its systems, its expectations, its categories, through which everything is to be categorized, measured and judged.

There also appears to be a persistent and widely held assumption that we have a better understanding of the world as a whole than previous generations have had. We observe and measure changes in society. We watch trends to detect change that is occurring so as to be able to extrapolate it into the future. We plan the future in line with such perceived trends. Thus, in the educational field, we are alert to birth rates, changing ethnicity of the population, employment statistics, and less quantifiable trends such as the growth of pluralism, the development of pressure groups, class conflict issues, technological change, and the state of international relations. If we believe that the quality of the future life of our society depends upon how such trends evolve and how we react to predicted trends, then education has a part to play and can help to make a difference in a desired direction. In this way we turn trends into intentions, and intentions into reality. This at least is the implicit theory of educational policy-making in contemporary western-style societies.

What, then, is the basis for this attitude of self-assurance or conviction that the West continues to have something, as valuable as it is intangible, to offer to the world? There is of course no one answer to this question, since it refers to the whole course of western culture in its formation and development, but an illustrative response can perhaps be made by taking the two major strands of secular rationalism that have emerged in modern western societies, Marxism and liberal–humanism, in order to examine their contributions to educational thinking and development.

The Marxist view

Although much day-to-day social analysis is of the kind in which social planning is adjusted to perceived trends, modern social sciences are more concerned with interpretation and explanation than with mere correlation. Since the development of positivist social science, it has been the dream of social analysts to understand the dynamics of society and to offer tools for its control and progress. This was the aim of Karl Marx in his system of ideas which, in the form of Marxism, has been the most ambitious, and perhaps hitherto the most successful of the progeny of 'social physics'. Marxism is an amalgam of disciplines, of economics, philosophy, sociology and psychology, which offers both prescriptions for social organization and explanations of social dynamics. It combines dispassionate analysis with moral fervour and sheer propaganda, since its acute economic observations are accompanied by political and moral commitment to the cause of the proletariat and by the vehement rejection of any belief in God.

There is enough social scientific evidence to indicate the validity of Marxists' perceptions of the existence of a social structure comprising classes with conflicting interests, and consequently of forces that systematically frustrate justice. For Marxists, education takes on essentially the same characteristics. The composition and structure of education reveals the same characteristics of division and conflict. The school system is socially stratified and reproduces social stratification. Powerful social interests use the schools both to confirm privilege on one class and to legitimize social and cultural disadvantage for another. The economy is reflected in the school which, wittingly or unwittingly, is its agent. Unless the school is radically reformed it can make no contribution to social progress, and yet educational reforms constantly fail through the lack of an adequate structural appraisal (Bowles and Gintis, 1976: 14). A further powerful contribution of Marxist thought to educational analysis has been made through the sociology of knowledge, in the work which seeks to explain correspondence of form between the economy and the very organization of the curriculum and its functions in reproducing social hierarchies (Williams, 1961; Bourdieu and Passeron, 1977).

In short, what we are given by Marxism is a radical critique of western education, of its overall structure, of its subservience to prevailing socio-economic interests, and of its unseen contradictions in enslaving the very minds of many of those it claims to be liberating because it differentiates largely in terms of the social characteristics which learners bring with them to school. Many works of Marxist inspiration which analyse such social functions of education offer little by way of a remedy, the implication being that it is not education that will change society, but a revolutionized society that will change education. Bowles and Gintis tell us that this is because, in terms of their 'correspondence theory', schools necessarily reflect the social order, and educational reforms fail through their failure to call into question basic structural conditions. Although they profess belief in 'an egalitarian and humanistic socialism', Bowles and Gintis do not believe that even radical proposals within education can address the major problems of society. They rest their hope upon the anachronism of social institutions becoming so apparent that the possibility of a 'democratic socialist movement bursting through' increases yearly (Bowles and Gintis, 1976: 14–15). In the meantime, they see the educational system as a kind of huge political football:

> Our objective for US schools and colleges here and now is not that they should become the embryo of the good society but that struggles around these institutions, and the educational process itself, should contribute to the development of a revolutionary, democratic socialist movement.
>
> (Bowles and Gintis, 1976: 269)

A comparable French study devotes itself to the detailed analysis of the way in which the primary school functions to reproduce the two-class structure of society, but its authors refuse to prescribe any remedy; this they say belongs not to them but to the wider political struggle (Beaudelot and Establet, 1971: 300).

Although British Marxists have not produced a work of the revolutionary vision of the Bowles and Gintis study, they have provided a growing corpus of studies of schools within their social structural context, as well as a wide range of studies of school organization which plot the success of the middle class in imposing and legitimizing their world-view. The main tenor is once again critical rather than creative. The principal curricular contribution made by Marxists is to propose social studies that inform learners about the social and economic conditions that affect their lives, in order both to encourage them to develop more egalitarian attitudes and to prepare them for protest. An exception, however, is found in Freire who, working in a Christian–Marxist perspective, has not concerned himself extensively with school curricula, but offers a curriculum and pedagogy in line with revolutionary principles. His exposition of the notion of conscientization has not been bettered, and many have found his programme of education for critical consciousness and humanization through co-intentional education and dialogue to be inspirational (Freire, 1972).

This is not the place for a general appraisal of the educational relevance of Marxism, except in so far as it represents the source of certain key ideas that constitute a major influence over education in western societies today which could distract us from, or erect barriers to, the spiritual. Whatever common ground may be found with Marxism in practice, those who adopt a fundamentally spiritual view of life must see in Marxist scientific materialism the denial of their essential beliefs. If all ideas, and ideals, are asserted to have a purely material or economic source, and if human progress is to depend essentially upon scientific and material progress, it is clear that this prescribes an educational system with no tolerance for a spiritual interpretation of life. Marxism presents us with a polarized vision of society, a class-based structure which can be dissolved only through conflict, intellectual, political or military. Education must reflect this belief – for belief it is.

The liberal–humanist view

The humanist tradition has been a powerful force in education in Britain, and indeed in France and the United States also. I am here thinking of those who believed that humanity could work towards its own perfection by relying upon pure reason. These were heirs to the Enlightenment. Their enquiries aim to be value-free. None the less, they have often sought to design ways by which humanity could be brought willingly under control; this was the avowed purpose of positivism in the mind of its founder, Comte, and this tradition was carried on in the republican ideals of the French school system in the nineteenth century (Prost, 1968). In their concern to attend only to what can be logically or empirically, and therefore publicly proved, humanists reject the religious view, which is seen as belonging to the private domain. However, despite the atheism espoused by rational humanists, Ward speaks of their 'religion of reason' (Ward, 1986: 23), and Prost recalls '*la foi laique*', the secularized religion of the primary school teachers of the Republic (Prost, 1968: 283–4); there is in fact a kind of worship of humanity and of human intelligence involved in this thinking. However self-righteous and arrogant it may have appeared during its progressive development over the past century, this was a noble tradition. Morality, genetic improvement, interpersonal and international relations could all be modelled and promoted through human reason, and only by human reason. Indeed, what are known as the humanistic therapies and psychologies, which are mainly of American origin, derive in part from such rational humanist thinking, as can be seen in atheistic reflections in the work of Fromm and Rogers, and in their belief in human perfectability (Fromm, 1966: 200; Rogers, 1983, chapter 13). However, these latter approaches are more comprehensive in their definitions of what counts as human, and include affective and physical elements. For this reason they will be discussed in relation to holistic paradigms in Chapter four, rather than in the context of rational–scientific thinking.

In its modern form of liberal–humanism, rationalism has played a major part in the development of western educational systems. In the context of the industrial revolution, liberal reformers, despite the later questioning of their motives, must be credited with laying the foundations for contemporary mass education. I defined the liberal–humanist viewpoint in education elsewhere, in the following terms:

> It involves a concern to find reasonable solutions to other people's problems, moral and social issues, and for understanding others' needs, interests and points of view. There is a commitment to pluralism and tolerance, and a questioning of all stereotyping. People are seen as equals.... There is an interest in global concerns..., and an unease about material values that might put things before people... there is a concern for seeing teaching as liberating, as a dialogue about ideas and values that expands awareness.
>
> (Plunkett, 1988: 2)

Holders of liberal and pluralist attitudes and values see the moral superiority of their approach as lying in its capacity to attach value to the free expression of other views than their own. This equality of rights, as interpreted in liberal philosophy, is increasingly given legislative force as well as being continually worked out in cultural and political discourse. Naturally, adherents of such systems are agnostic on philosophical and religious points which do not counter the pluralist system. In Berger's terms, modernity has imposed upon everybody the 'heretical imperative', that is the requirement to make a personal choice of the position from which they understand reality, because no one view can any longer command universal assent (Berger, 1980). Far from being a matter of regret, it is a common liberal contention that a greater truth emerges from conflict, so that a positive value is ascribed to intellectual and political conflict at least.

The characteristic values of liberalism in education throughout modern western society have thus been those of the superiority of rational enquiry over dogmatic authority, the right to freedom of thought and speech, and to equality of opportunity and choice in school and society. Furthermore, education is regarded as leading to a wide range of recognizable outcomes, not all of which are subject to measurement. Personal development and moral values, as well as the capacity to form and develop positive human relationships, are widely acknowledged as desirable aims of education, and although these themes run through the huge span of contemporary educational and curricular policies in western society, there are few efforts to discern and advocate what precise values should prevail. Educational institutions rarely approach curriculum reappraisal through a thorough process of identifying criteria and purposes (DES, 1983: 7), and it can even be asked whether a rationalist position allows for what is necessarily a subjective as opposed to a provable proposition. When a group of French General Inspectors was asked to produce a set of basic educational values they reported in a characteristically rationalist expression that: 'Moral education is strictly a logical impossibility in a national lay state educational service.' ('Combats contre les Ombres', *Documentation Française*, May 1981, quoted in Mourral, 1984: 76.)

None the less, many liberal thinkers have contended that they were themselves value-free in their educational prescriptions. Hirst laments the fact that, 'the schools are not even in principle committed to the demands of open, critical, rational education in (religious education and moral education)' (Hirst, 1985: 15). The point has been reached where there is a fear of belief and commitment on account of suspicions of indoctrination, and yet even the relativism of the values expressed do constitute a belief. In a valiant theoretical effort sustained over many years, Hirst and other British philosophers of education have argued for an objective structure to the curriculum based upon an irreducible number of forms of knowledge which demand consequently to be sampled by all learners. In fact this structure mirrors traditional academic practice in Britain, and it was carried forward in the late 1970s by Her Majesty's Inspectorate which virtually placed their corporate authority behind the nine 'areas of learning and experience' that should be included in an adequate school curriculum. These were usually listed in alphabetical order, as follows: aesthetic/creative ethical, linguistic, mathematical, physical, scientific, social/political, spiritual (DES, 1977, Supplement) and, added later, technological (DES, 1985b). Most other major contributions to curriculum design in the liberal–humanist tradition in England have been variations on this theme, either recognizing the separate forms or areas, or looking for ways to bind and blend them.

The fact that these prescriptions were not as objective as had been thought, and could not carry total conviction, is evident from comparisons that can be made with other societies which place less emphasis upon theoretical and academic education, or which seek to develop closer links between school and adult, or community education, and working life. The truth of this was borne in at an official level upon educational institutions and curriculum planners in Britain by the development of alternative curricula and pedagogies, especially with the introduction from the late 1970s of new programmes for pre-vocational education in schools and colleges of further education. These have placed much more reliance upon a general core of education, integrating a range of academic learning, skills and attitudes through a pedagogy that was substantially more experiential in character than was the practice of the traditional school. It thus appears that what are believed to be value-free educational prescriptions can become as doctrinaire as dogmas they aim to replace. Structurally enforced submission to the authority of the philosopher or educational scientist, which has occurred mainly through assessment mechanisms in Britain, can cripple and imprison the unconventional teacher who is seeking to work within another paradigm.

What has been called 'rational curriculum development' has exhibited this fore-ordained character. There is a sense in which first principles have been forgotten or ignored, and the whole system is replete with the taken-for-granted. Universities in Britain are a case in point. Do they have a philosophy guiding their development? Despite rigorous criticism from Government and industry for many years, British universities have found no defence more effective than to try to do more of what they are told by industry and Government. There has been very little evidence that modern universities know why they exist, why they need to exist as something different from other social institutions, towards which destination they are going, or towards which they want to lead society. The damning indictment of American universities made by Allan Bloom is surely valid for Britain. Academic activity has been corralled, tamed, vocationalized, and the only arguments now offered for university education are of a special pleading character, to defend particular disciplines or privileges. Bloom rather nobly asserts that the college years are civilization's only chance to get to the student, but that this programme fails because of the agnosticism of the university. A 'democracy of the disciplines' (Bloom, 1988: 337) constitutes a kind of anarchy, or a set of competing visions in which no view is authoritative, and where, he alleges, as has already been quoted, 'there is no synopsis'.

The strength of modern scholarship lies precisely in the division of learning into specializations, and the penetrating development of knowledge into more and more focussed sub-specialisms. Apart from the philosophical tradition which I have been discussing, there are the scientific and social scientific groupings of disciplines which can broadly be called empirical. While, as we have already seen, the scientific world-view tends to dismiss ideas of purpose in the world, and to set spiritual, religious, and sometimes even moral values aside, an even more generalized relativism has characterized the social sciences. Totally contradictory theories, such as those associated with behaviourist and cognitive psychology, are simultaneously held and applied in schools and society. The apotheosis of this approach has been to enthrone methodology as the queen of the sciences in the place of philosophy – or theology as Newman contended. Education comes to consist of observing what is happening, even stirring the pot to watch, and record, the result. The personal and creative dimensions of learning are neglected, and to an even greater degree the notion of knowledge as anything other than an interminable process of enquiry is repudiated.

A rational view of education cannot stand by itself. It is enmired in a values agnosticism in which a logical, rather than a moral coherence is being sought. This leads to the sterility of the neutral school or curriculum, that is a learning situation in which no one is allowed to take a genuine moral stand, except as an exercise. Education is a process for sorting out facts and ideas, dealing fairly with controversy, which is to say not deciding issues and values, let alone beliefs. 'We set our hopes on human reason,' as Ward puts it, 'and human reason is not enough to save us from passion and power, greed and envy' (Ward, 1986: 23). The final paradox is, as Bloom puts it, that 'what is advertised as a great opening is a great closing' (Bloom, 1988: 34). This is because openness is carried to such lengths that commitment is excluded. The mind is closed to values. It is never time to choose, to be counted, actually to do what is good or right.

The limits of the rationalist view in education

While the adherents of Marxist and liberal–humanist approaches may be contrasted in the strength of their doctrines and convictions, the first for its dogmatic stance, and the second for its reasoning and negotiating characteristics, both take a global perspective from which they can turn their enquiries to any subject. Rationalists can analyse metaphysics; they can seek to understand alchemy; they can understand the dynamics of primitive kinship systems; they can even generate models and explanations of human instincts, emotions and values. In this sense, rationalists are self-sufficient. Their science, their interpretation of data, their logic can take everything into account. Why then do rationalists not give us the truth? Why do they not agree? Why do we find that we can simply talk about them without necessarily feeling involved? How is it possible to respect rationalists while simultaneously, and without condescension, pitying them? How well founded is the confidence of rationalists? How comprehensive is their view of reality?

What, in sum, has been the impact of rationalist enquiry and proposals upon education? The principal implication of liberal humanism has been to make the intellect pre-eminent, and to attach value to conceptual thinking or abstract forms of knowledge, detached from everyday usefulness. A further consequence is that we have an educational system, one which enthrones intelligence, success and especially individual brilliance. It enshrines the open mind, but is contemptuous of all who do not accept its own criteria for the worthwhile. It thus in effect imposes its own creed and creates the demand for its own rituals, such as examinations, tests and specialist publications. Education in this rationalist mode neglects the inner self, the emotions and the physical being in all but the most superficial ways, by acknowledging them conceptually but not experientially. The cost to our overall well-being may be high. Reviewing the clinical conclusions of Jung's work, his assistant Aniela Jaffe comments: 'One-sided over-valuation of rational consciousness and of an ego-dominated world, as well as vitiation of instinct, lie at the root of many neuroses and psychic illnesses in modern man' (Jaffe, 1975: 93–4).

The materialistic perspective of Marxist thought, while capable of generating educational programmes, has mainly been exploited to attack education in capitalist societies as an ideological instrument for maintaining the socio-economic status quo. Starting from the conviction that only the pursuing of class conflict can improve the lot of humanity, Marxism breeds a certain kind of irrationality. Conflict begets conflict. The obsession with material growth leads first to the control and then to the destruction of the environment. No one can prove that Marxist theory is wrong. The matter is an empirical one. But neither could it be proved right except in some putative later stage of life on the planet. In the meantime, it constitutes a belief system, a set of concepts which stand for experience. It does not have the authority of experience, as does, for example, the awareness that the personal experience of sharing is in some sense more valid than the mere concept of equality. Nor can it explain or justify commitment, and thus what Marxists or indeed other believers do may reflect a greater human, and indeed spiritual, value than the belief they profess. In educational terms, Marxism must indoctrinate, not merely put its tenets forward but impose them regardless of the disposition of mind of the learner.

It tends also to be the case that the rational acts as a self-fulfilling prophecy: so powerful is its persuasive force of argument that it can alter people's expectations and aspirations. It affects the longer-term future by its predictions and proposals for priorities. Such effects of rational thinking and planning are not necessarily harmful, of course, since they can help societies to achieve control over the development and impact of the educational system in line with whatever purposes it may have.

57

However, it is clear that a curriculum based upon rational assumptions is constrained by the scope of the assumptions made. Formal models of the curriculum that rely upon rational knowledge structures cannot take account of experiential, intuitive or creative learning. Curricular programmes determined in advance by rational calculation tend to deflect attention from individual students' needs and motivation. Rational principles built into educational systems over time tend also to be inflexible in the face of new or changing political priorities. Above all, the requirements of nationally planned system- wide educational programmes can abridge minority rights and deny individual preferences in the spiritual and religious spheres.

What characterizes all these variations of the rationalist approach is the assumption that human beings are best able to deal with issues and problems by thinking, perhaps also by communicating with each other. The extent to which these processes work can, however, only be shown retrospectively. Along the way we see only clashes of values, polarization of viewpoints, scepticism, relativism, and resistance to any openness to an absolute. We cannot know rationally whether there is any better way of looking at things. In other words, however successful rationality may be in answering its own questions about causes and purposes, it cannot fill the spiritual gap. It cannot answer the ultimate questions about why we exist, or what purposes the universe and its inhabitants may serve. In this sense, it cannot claim to be comprehensive, and thus it is observable that many choose to pursue their existential enquiries outside of rational analysis and discourse, looking rather to insight and illumination from non-rational sources such as the arts, religion and the world of everyday experience.

Rationalism and the spiritual

There is no point in a lengthy discussion in this book of what it might mean to assert that there is no God, and how far we might get in reaching a rational consensus about the world, or about education, on that basis. That is a task for others if they want to undertake it. Rationalism is being discussed here as a partial view of reality, as an essentially atheistic *a priori*. Its reality in fact ends with the human mind, which means that it leaves entirely out of account the possibility of a Creator who has given humanity the basis for its existence, for evolution, for morality and the purposes of human life. This does not mean, of course, that rationalist thinking is not of value to the theist. It is, so long as it is commonly accepted that we have a material and a mental world to deal with. And there is no question but that rationalism as a part of that existence is extremely important in understanding the human world we live in, and even the world of religion, which has been so influenced by rationalism during the past two centuries.

Reason can make apparent sense out of certain public manifestations of the spiritual, such as practices of self-discipline, charitable inclinations, or principles of conduct, as in the universal adages: do to others as you would be done by, or, behave only in such a way as can be taken as a general norm, but in the end scientific rationality is obliged to impose its own criteria of meaning and explanation which belong to the public domain (Trigg, 1973: 17). We are then left with the notion either of a God who can only be known subjectively, or the 'God of the gaps', that is, where the religious and the spiritual are confined to those areas into which reason has not yet extended its searchlight. These, however, are seen as constantly diminishing in number and in significance (Davies, 1984, chapter 1). Thus there is what I would regard as a spurious route from the rational to the spiritual which is quite commonly found, but which in fact treats the spiritual in a mundane and compromised manner. This approach is represented in Figure 1 by category F. For example, the way that spiritual commitments are interpreted politically by non-adherents, and possibly by some adherents also, as in the case of the civil status and mission associated with the organized churches, is to restrict to a cultural form what church members take to be in its essence the result of divine influence. This has led to the development of what has been called 'civil religion' (Glock and Bellah, 1976), which is the outcome of a process of the progressive secularization of religion (Berger, 1980: 108).

In parallel, social-scientific interpretation of religious behaviour and phenomena subjects the religious and spiritual domains to the disciplines of the social sciences. Such viewpoints are sustainable within their frames of reference, but they are necessarily reductionist with regard to any presumed spiritual, let alone divine dimension to reality. This desire to give a prominent status to reason, or what Hervieu-Léger calls 'hegemonic rationalism' (Hervieu-Léger, 1986: 156), can also be so absorbed by the adherents of the spiritual view that they become preoccupied with how to reconcile their aspirations with the rational. Examples would be the development of the doctrine of 'prosperity theology' or the the exploration of situational ethics. Here the would-be spokesmen for the spiritual view become the allies of the rationalists and even atheists, as happened in the 1960s with 'death of God' theology. It was, to say the least, paradoxical to postulate a death of God theology, but this represented the ultimate in accommodating the spiritual to rational, material and worldly viewpoints. This strain of the utilitarian and the rational within the religious camp, however, remains active and widespread. It is found in some aspects of liberation theology and in those tendencies within contemporary moral theology which seem effectively to subordinate the spiritual to purely analytical or ideological positions, solutions or criteria of conduct. Newbigin gives the example of the liberal theologians who are driven to seeing the resurrection of Jesus Christ as a psychological experience of the disciples. Faith and reason have become conflated.

The unacknowledged beliefs of would-be rationalists, whether of the liberal or Marxist persuasion, end by undermining faith in human reason (Ward, 1986: 22–3). Liberal relativism and Marxist dogmatism both fail the criterion of open-mindedness. Both ignore the deeply personal level, and the significance of personal beliefs and values. Both fend off the need for a God. Both raise the issue of freedom, but leave us wondering: freedom for what? Both encourage only scepticism because they offer nothing that we can grasp at the existential level, no immediate truth, no meaning, no principles of life. The implications for education of this failure were spoken of by Maritain as a '*mal métaphysique*', that is, the refusal of the rationalists to face responsibilities in the area of values, and thus:

> ...the total vacuum of any kind of absolute value and any kind of faith in the truth in which the young are placed by the prevailing intelligentsia, and by a school and university education which largely and cavalierly betrays its essential mission.
>
> (Maritain, 1969: 119)

The resigned 'What is truth?' of Pontius Pilate stands for the attitude of so many who have given up hope of knowing anything for certain through reason or science. One person's truth is another's hypothesis to be tested. Scepticism is a moral obligation. What seems true one moment, as Kuhn shows, is no longer seen to be valid the next (Kuhn, 1970). We place our trust in a way of thinking, an ideology which empowers us, convinces us for a time, and then, like a balloon, bursts leaving us with nothing. It is easier to ignore the notion that there is a divine power when the hard evidence does not confront us as clearly as it appears to in scientific enquiries, but this does not justify turning the religious message into a purely rational argument, because this cannot confer any more lasting validity on it.

The rationalist way, eschewing purposes and values, therefore fails, and secularism comes to be seen itself as a myth or, as Berger says, 'Secularism is in crisis today' (Berger, 1980: 184). The problem is that secularism not only leads to spiritual indifference, but it generates a relativistic attitude to moral values, and in the end leads to moral indifference within the secular society (Longley, 1988). I recently encountered an example of this in a senior, and apparently highly professional teacher of personal and social education who acknowledged that he could not bring himself to deal with Aids as a moral issue because, he said, he felt that would not fit the image of the kind of teacher he had become. If professional values can be so lightly set aside, there is no guarantee of wisdom for the kind of concentrated use of reason that we associate with scholarship; indeed all human thought forms have to find their way through 'yonder wicket gate' on the way to spiritual enlightenment.

Rationally we are compelled to admit that ultimate reality and truth could be illusions, that they may only exist as the product of our thought processes. Unless we are satisfied with pure solipsism we are driven to look for an alternative world-view. One alternative could be the spiritual level of existence of the eastern religions, and there is a fundamental difference between such understandings of reality and western rationalism. Or we could accept that what exists is the result of a creative design by the incomparably superior intelligence of God, and that the reality being studied by the scientific rationalists is only part of that creation, and a part that they will never be able to understand fully if they take it as all that exists. The rationalists who believe that reality comprises only what we know through our senses and intelligence are in fact making a god out of the universe. They are lending it, as an *a priori*, powers it does not have. As Tresmontant points out, the universe is constantly developing; it is constantly being created. Several billion years ago the universe was merely hydrogen with a bit of helium, and some traces of other elements being formed (Tresmontant, 1980). Where did the development and increase come from? This question is surely meaningful, and therefore answerable, only in the context of a dialogue between science and religion.

Chapter four

The holistic alternative

Crab: Holism is the most natural thing in the world to grasp. It's simply the belief that 'the whole is greater than the sum of its parts'. No one in his right mind could reject holism.
Anteater: Reductionism is the most natural thing in the world to grasp. It's simply the belief that 'a whole can be understood completely if you can understand its parts, and the nature of their "sum"'. No one in her left brain could reject reductionism.

(Hofstadter, 1982: 162)

Rather than through pursuing the rational line, there may be greater potential for human growth from the new reflection upon the holistic in medical, scientific and other disciplines, including education (Bohm, 1981; Capra, 1983; Davies, 1984). The fragmentation of knowledge, relationships, and of purposes, is widely felt to have reached extreme proportions, and the struggle back towards common outlooks and values seems essential for our survival. Many have intuited this, and their desire has been to find a route, a basis for a more comprehensive way of looking at reality. The intellectual history of the past couple of generations has been of this search, by only a few at first, because the problem had not been widely recognized, and now by a whole flood of people with increasing confidence, some seeing themselves as prophets of a new age (Ferguson, 1982).

Less self-consciously, a whole popular experience was leading to parallel discoveries. The 1960s appeared to mark the death throes in the western world of traditional Christianity, a faith hitherto transmitted by the family and, even if abandoned, rarely seriously questioned as a cultural force. The cultural explosion of that decade, however, was one that virtually jettisoned the past. Young people were becoming disconnected from cultural and moral traditions, as witness the growth of scepticism and satire turned upon all authority in those years. It was the same throughout western society and its organizations, including the churches. The first stage of the search was for individual freedom, for identity, for self-justification. This was the era of civil rights agitation, the birth of causes of all kinds, democratization, participation, equality of opportunity. There was an ideological profusion, but little solid foundation, little linkage of issues (Marcuse, 1972). The hippies were one category of people who began to look for some more underlying truths that could bind people together. Some eschewed capitalist values while inhabiting capitalist societies for the most part. Others abandoned their own cultures to search far away, and began a cult of the East, looking for answers in old faiths, but remote ones. This was a naive movement of blind hope, and yet it has left a residue, a kind of modern metaphysic, which has helped many to find alternatives to rational, logically systematized ways of living, such as the diversified new-age cults that have originated mainly in the western states of the US in recent years.

For many of us the holistic is the fruit of the 1960s, of the protest movements against an overly technological view of the world, including the technologies of social control through discrimination, war and political oppression. However, we can now see that there has been no simple transition to a holistic consensus. The more our societies explored alternatives, the more resistance grew, so that we now have a highly polarized situation: the pragmatic rationalist, essentially reductionist view as opposed to the holistic. It is therefore necessary to explore in some detail the nature of this polarity, and the insights it generates for education.

Themes in holistic awareness

In science

Although I could not hope to discuss the notion of the holistic comprehensively here, any more than I could do justice to the rational in the previous chapter, I need to ensure some common understanding, or at least that a reader should be able to grasp what I mean by the term as it is being used to denote the second circle, particularly in relation to the 'intuitive' category B, of the Map of the Values Terrain in Figure 1. The task of this chapter is thus to ensure that the concept of the holistic is sufficiently marked off from the areas of awareness indicated by 'rational' and 'spiritual' in this book. The subject is vast, and recent developments are diverse, but the problem was aptly summed up by Aldous Huxley decades ago when he wrote:

> We are both intellect and passion, our minds have both objective knowledge of the outer world and subjective experience. To discover methods of bringing these separate worlds together, to show the relationship between them, is, I feel, the most important task of modern education.
>
> (Huxley, 1980: 15)

To assess how far this task may have progressed in recent times would be another way of describing the purpose of this chapter, but it is also necessary to recognize how widely the holistic paradigm has diffused in recent years.

It is Bohm's view that it is essential to fuse the objective and the subjective, because our ways of perceiving the external world are not the same as the reality of that world; they are merely partial accounts (Bohm, 1981: 4–5). Our theory or concepts necessarily determine what we will perceive when we examine the world. Since it has been the characteristic of the sciences that they have divided up the world and catalogued reality to be able to study it, there is the danger that we imagine reality to be as fragmented as our ways of apprehending it. 'Wholeness is what is real', Bohm avers (Bohm, 1981: 7). Both Bohm and Capra trace the emergence of an organic view of reality from the mechanical model bequeathed to us by traditional science. Both are physicists, and use their discipline as the exemplar while maintaining that the wholeness of reality includes not merely ways of knowing, but the knower and the known as well. The alternative to this would be the self-assertion which would deny the whole, whereas the whole is viable only if the individual submits to integration within it (Capra, 1983: 27). This idea is paralleled by Bohm's contention that a view of the whole situation is needed if we are to understand details; science can no longer begin from the details in order to build a world-view. He gives the example of the stream with its multiple eddies and vortices. We are obliged to start from the concept of the whole stream if we are to understand the vortices (Bohm, 1981: 18–19).

In his exploratory study, Capra contrasts two paradigms, the Newtonian and the organic. He traces the Newtonian model through biology, medicine, psychology and economics, and suggests the counter-model of organic wholeness, that is:

> ...based on awareness of the essential interrelatedness and interdependence of all phenomena – physical, biological, psychological, social, and cultural.
>
> (Capra, 1983: 285)

Writing on the Big Sur coast of California in the early 1980s, he virtually answers the questions that Huxley was raising at Santa Barbara two decades earlier. He shows ways that it may be possible to re-draw the map of knowledge as a single canvas rather than as a multiplicity of separated disciplines, which Huxley saw as subject to the 'celibacy of the intellect' (Huxley, 1980: 13). The reference is to the autonomy, even mutual avoidance of academic specializations, the compartmentalization of work, and the consequent fragmentation of reality.

Capra defines the holistic as referring to an understanding of reality in terms of integrated wholes whose properties cannot be reduced to those of smaller units, and these wholes will in turn be parts of larger wholes. This is what Koestler's notion of the holon recognizes, but the holon has the additional property that it both serves an integrative function as a part of a larger whole and a self-assertive function to preserve its own autonomy. 'In a healthy system there is a balance between integration and self-assertion' (Capra, 1983: 27). Bohm takes us further into the understanding of the holistic with his comparison of the lens which can view only a specific aspect of an object, and the hologram, which can make a photographic record of the interference pattern of light waves that have come off the object (Bohm, 1981: 145–47). Each part of the record contains information about the whole original object. The form and structure of the entire object are enfolded within each region of the record, and light shone on any particular part of the record reveals an image of the whole object (Bohm, 1981: 177).

This is a powerful image of the holistic, since it suggests that we may not always have to look at the widest level of reality to understand the whole. The whole may be understood by examining the part, provided that we are consciously and deliberately seeking to learn about the whole. One man tells us about humanity, one branch tells us about forests, and one chromosome can, in some sense, tell us about a person. Bohm goes on to discuss other ways in which the reality we are dealing with in everyday life and in science of the conventional kind are of what he calls the 'explicate order', whereas the understanding of that reality belongs fundamentally to an 'implicate order', that is, the wholeness from which separateness derives (Bohm, 1981: 147 ff.). If this concept can be shown to be rationally meaningful in science, as Bohm claims it is, it immediately encourages us to see such science as the explicate order of a larger implicate whole, a system whose properties are not necessarily material or physical, that is, a universal system of which the material and physical are only a part.

As an example of what we might discover, a particular poem might tell us about the physical world, the mind of the poet and the beauty of the world. The poem is a holon. Similarly, a verse of the Bible may in some sense contain its essential truth, as has always been believed by mystics, like the Russian Orthodox monks who repeat a phrase a thousand times over in a day as a distillation of spiritual truth. Thus the 'pearl of great price' is, at the same time, image and reality. If we stay faithfully with the image, we come to know the truth it contains. So I am arguing that the physicist illuminates the whole of reality, including spiritual reality, as does the poem, the gospel parable or the verse of the psalm. However, not all these processes are as immediately productive for our purposes as others. The hologram is obviously efficient for physical and visual images, the poem for aesthetic and affective understandings, and the Bible verse for expanding our awareness of spiritual reality.

The organic and the personal

The theme of the organic opens up an even wider view of the holistic than such scientific work reflects, because it contains the essential idea of the interrelatedness of parts and the whole, and the correlate of the meaninglessness of parts without the whole. If I take a simple example from everyday life, as I look out of my window at a rhododendron bush I seem to see oranges where I know in reality there are only yellowing leaves. How do I explain this? Is it just a mistake of poor eyesight and a trick of the afternoon light? Is it an error caused by not having my rational faculties in control? Is it a mere flight of imagination, a desire for the exotic while I undergo the discipline of my keyboard? Is it a sign of my subconscious enthusiasm for a forthcoming trip to Israel? Is it a waking symbolic dream about fruitfulness in life? I need not go on; the point is simply that the explanation can never be given, but it could well be to do with all these factors, and hundreds more. And it is the synthesis of elements that provides the greater truth, scientific or not. Thus, the phenomenon is holistic in the sense that it would be pointless to examine the leaf to study how well it resembles an orange; I would never have entertained the idea of the orange unless the leaf had been partly hidden in a deep green bush, to be sure, but there also had to be the predisposing psychological factors that brought that particular image to mind.

Whereas in the previous chapter we were concerned with the efforts of the human mind to analyse and understand reality as a separate phenomenon, we now have to acknowledge the problem that consciousness itself has some of the features of material reality in its dynamic movement; its sharply distinct successive cameos of the world are not themselves the reality they reflect. Thoughts glance off each other continuously, and this movement is more important than the frozen image of an idea. Not only is the analysis frozen, but it is restricted to the rational lens, whereas many other lenses are imaginable. In particular, the affective understanding and the physical sensing of reality give access to alternative sources of data. Our consciousness of reality comes not only from our minds, but from our hearts and bodies, and thus there are many other ways of knowing apart from the activity of our minds. Concurrent with our thoughts, we have instincts, interpersonal rapport, conditioning, empathy, emotions, senses, and perhaps other modes of perceiving that we hint at with such expressions as intuitions, hunches, sixth sense, and so forth.

Once we have accepted the potential diversity of the inputs into our human awareness that come from our nature and the different contexts within which we can conceive ourselves to exist, it is no longer possible to accept the notion of the disembodied intellect as more than a figment of the imagination. The systemic, planned, controlled and predictable part of our consciousness or learning can only be an infinitesimal proportion of what we know as individuals, and then we have to take account of society and history which affect us in unaccountable ways, through our thoughts, emotions, values, physical well-being and biological evolution. And yet that incredible diversity has a unity, at the very least at the level of the individual person. One of the interviews contained in Robinson's study *The Original Vision* illustrates this very powerfully:

> I believe that a child has a wholeness. Looking back, it seems to me that I was whole in the sense that I was not yet disturbed by the sorrows that came later, at school. I was open, therefore, to receive. That simple wholeness is something like the wholeness of an animal, but more conscious perhaps. I would compare that simple wholeness with the more complex wholeness that you work towards slowly. I think I am much more whole today at 81 than I was at 40. And perhaps when a new wholeness has been achieved out of the complexities of life, one will be able to see the world invisible again.
>
> (Robinson, 1975: 52)

Our total consciousness, which must include what is called our unconscious, thus multiplies the dimensions of reality which are effective in our lives, even though we are not able to inspect its contents in a systematic, or even fully conscious, manner. As Jung puts it, 'people identify themselves almost exclusively with their consciousness, and imagine that they are only what they know about themselves' (Jung, 1974: 330).

Jung has made a major contribution to our understanding of human wholeness by his model of the four functions of the personality. Each person has in their consciousness a dominant function of either thinking, feeling, intuition or sensation, and another of these as a supporting function. The other two functions then tend to be repressed in the unconscious, and constitute the main forces of the shadow self. Because the shadow self is directed to quite different ends from the conscious self, it appears that internal conflicts, neuroses and other such manifestations are harmful to the personality, but Jung sees the unconscious as making a potentially positive contribution to personal development through the broadening of consciousness in knowledge, creativity and spiritual awareness. The fullest realization of the self comes from the resolution of the struggle between the conscious and unconscious forces, and can occur only when the individual has become aware of his or her shadow self. Laurens van der Post, who was a close friend of

Jung, and who was interested in how he sought wholeness in his own life, interprets his thinking as follows:

> Man could only be well and sane when the quarrel between him and his shadow, between the primitive and the civilised, was dissolved. Only when the two were reconciled could they enter together into the presence of the master-pattern, as Jung's experience had already done. Only then did man become whole. Wholeness was the ultimate of man's conscious and unconscious seeking.
>
> (van der Post, 1978: 218)

One of the major conflicts of this kind that affects the human personality stems from the coexistence in the psyche of masculine and feminine principles. The 'anima', or feminine principle, is seen by Jung as 'the inner feminine figure in the male', and it corresponds to those characteristics and qualities associated especially with the feminine (Jung, 1974: 210). If this is denied, then male values are dominant and unquestioned, but if a feminine–masculine spectrum of values is recognized, a greater integration of self is attained. Although the issue of feminism in contemporary society and culture, including education, is worthy of treatment in depth in a work on the holistic, it must be acknowledged as of enormous importance for the theme of the spiritual in this work. It is the anima that expresses the need, which is internal to the unconscious, to balance the forces of rational thought and the intuitive. Feminist themes of cooperative and collective social organization, care of the person and the environment, creating space for feelings and senses, can be seen as part of the rebellion of our own natures against rational–scientific obsessions of modern western culture.

There are three further extensions to this view of wholeness at the personal level which are significant for our present purposes. The first is that since our understanding is physically embodied, many of our modes of knowing are experiential. Another way of looking at this is to say that a mind that ignores or distrusts experience is wilfully destroying the evidence. Subjective experience of reality causes us to question the scientific empiricism on which so much of our formal knowledge is based. There is a difference between experiment and experience, in the sense that one process is characterized by the formal search for expected outcomes, while the other is open to the as yet unimagined. Contemporary physicists speak of the fundamental link between the observer and the observed, while sociologists recognize the structural features of the ownership of ideas and perceptions. The validity of the detached view, the subjection of external reality to human dominance or controls through rational planning, measurement and technological manipulation has to be reviewed in the light of immediate experience and the awareness that where we stand and the way we look at the world determine what we see. I am reminded of the incident of the American anthropologist who had the idea of giving a reservation Indian instructions in the use of a movie camera, and asked him to film a tribal ceremony. The result was a long sequence of shots all showing the to-ings and fro-ings of a man collecting together the ritual instruments and preparing the setting, massively repetitive, 'boring' and 'meaningless' – a long way from the 'somebody has something, and somebody else wants it' story-line of countless Hollywood chase scenes!

The second point of extension of which only brief mention will be made in this chapter is the modes of knowing that some believe are available through paranormal or spiritual communications. It is clear that this is a very significant area of awareness, because there are people who actually determine the whole pattern of their lives, and even attitudes towards their deaths, by the faith they place in such knowledge. It enters our daily lives not only in the form of traditional religious observances but also in the search for special knowledge and enlightenment through, among other ways, dreams, the occult, astrology, communication with spirits, the use of hallucinogenic drugs, and the practice of disciplines such as yoga and transcendental meditation.

Finally, there is the view taken by the practitioners of holistic health, which comprises a family of disciplines that recognize the body, mind and spirit as forming one whole, and needing therefore to be treated as a unity (Pietroni, 1986). The tension between conventional and alternative, or complementary, medicine reveals only that the holistic paradigm is not widely accepted in society, so that the established medical confraternity is able to ignore the case made for it, whether in the area of diagnosis or treatment. It is thus not surprising that nurses are showing much greater interest than most doctors in holistic health care and in the strategies for prevention and sharing of responsibility with the patient that it entails (Holmes, 1984). Increasingly, however, doctors are looking for ways to combine traditional and complementary approaches. One consultant with a specialism in rehabilitation illustrated the holistic approach with reference to back pain, when he spoke of the holistic as (a) contrasted with the traditional, (b) natural rather than processed, (c) with every factor given equal hearing, and (d) as having a spiritual component.[1] According to the traditional reductionist medical model, back pain would be studied mechanically and as a syndrome. However, different medical specialisms could take contradictory views, some favouring physical treatment, some drugs, some psychological approaches. A holistic approach might begin with studying how patients treat their backs, looking at the matter either ergonomically or in terms of lifestyle, so that it is likely that in the end patients would be contributing to generating their own treatment.

The ecological

The interrelationship seen between mind and matter provides a further extension of the holistic health idea. Roszak, in his book *Person/Planet* sees the earth and the individual as having the same needs (Roszak, 1981). Human survival is ecological as well as psychological. Humanity cannot continue to harden its divisions into sexes, races and classes, and hope to survive. There is a need for a wholeness that is culturally and morally inclusive. This sense of global wholeness is a modern phenomenon related obviously to the way that technology has shrunk the world, but it does not follow that humanity accepts the 'moral universe' of which Thomas Merton wrote (Merton, 1949: 12). One writer puts this point succinctly. He suggests that the world is evolving to become both 'synchronic' and 'anomic' (Ferrarotti, 1984: 14). I take this to mean that we are all living within a mutually contingent reality, in touch with each other at least potentially in so many different ways across the globe, but we are not accepting the same moral and cultural imperatives, so our very contingency is producing the tensions that threaten our survival. Apart from the overwhelming facts of terrorism, war and threats of wars that are the main diet of the world's media, it is perhaps in the ecological field that the lessons of the holistic are most being registered. Writing about public consciousness of erosion, Jonathan Porritt, director of Friends of the Earth, expresses it thus: 'All living creatures are inextricably linked together,...every wound inflicted on the earth is therefore a wound inflicted on ourselves' (Porritt, 1986). But he argues that this is being 'kept out of sight and out of mind', presumably by anomic and exploitative interests, when the need is for more and more people to participate in finding solutions.

Although it lays claim in one sense to universality, western rationalism is also socially and culturally located. People in certain social positions, with particular needs and opportunities, tend to see the world within a common rational framework. But who is to say that this is more universal than the view of those who search for the meaning and purpose of life in terms of emotional needs, physical sensations or spiritual forces? Many cultures in the world, predominantly in the East, place far less emphasis than the rational West upon practical effectiveness, efficiency, production, private ownership, systematic organization and similar shibboleths. Capra suggests that what is needed is a synthesis of West and East, rational control and intuitive openness, so that the self-sufficiency of rational thinking is held in check. The area in which this balancing factor is most needed, according to Capra, is in what he refers to as 'deep ecology':

> Which is rooted in a perception of reality that goes beyond the scientific framework to an intuitive awareness of the oneness of all life, the interdependence of its multiple manifestations and its cycles of change and transformation.
>
> (Capra, 1983: 458)

It is obvious that the more we subject reality to rational control, that is, the more we extend our conceptualizations, categorizations, rules and predictions, the less we can hope to be informed by personal insights, intuitions, relationships, serendipity and non-defensive openness. The rational social order of tolerant democracy has its value, for sure, but its very relativism tends to exclude qualities of commitment, belief and explosive cultural change, along with other more questionable forms of illumination. Indeed, the failure to allow for what Ehrenzweig called the 'hidden order of art', the implicit knowledge of forms and forces on which creative work must draw, is one of the most demonstrable penalties of exclusive rationalism (Ehrenzweig, 1970). Above all, God has been excluded, whereas in holistic world-views, necessarily syntheses of eastern and western wisdom, a variety of hypotheses about God are encountered. For Capra, deep ecology has spiritual and religious affinities, which are reinforced by the kinship he sees between feminism and ecology (Capra, 1983: 458ff.).

Holistic education

It will not have escaped the reader's attention that virtually the whole profusion of concepts and ideas in the general discussion of the first half of this chapter have a ready application to the educational field. In one sense this is obvious, and yet it is hard to point to a single work that carries the holistic insight fruitfully and penetratingly into the world of modern education. Classical writers had holistic insights, of course, and we could easily find them in the works of the Greeks, in Rousseau, Froebel and Montessori, or in such near contemporaries as Russell, Steiner and Neill. But the challenge now is to incorporate the contributions of contemporary scientists, psychologists, therapists and social scientists into an appropriate understanding of what education could be in the future. I am not myself aiming to attempt this, as I have what is for me an even more important objective, but I would like to see it done, and I hope that the next few pages may go some way towards indicating what I see as a possible agenda for the work.

Chapter two considered the pragmatic character of much current

71

public curriculum policy, which is bound to continue to affect curriculum design in the forseeable future. The basis for the kind of rational curriculum planning referred to in Chapter three, however, was seen to lie in a notion of largely objective knowledge which was either structured in itself, in what were seen as irreducible forms, or assimilable through a structured process of learning, such as the nine areas of experience and learning. This rational approach tended to concentrate upon the human being as learner, as mind. The experience of the curriculum as essentially a cognitive one. The whole western liberal and rational tradition of education has the bias of the academic, the empirically verifiable, the logical.

Holistic education, by contrast, is education not only of the mind, but of the whole person, body, mind and spirit, and also of the person in community, and this within a context of knowledge seen as the proverbial seamless robe. The role of the teacher is less to be a source of information and ideas than a guide towards enriched methods of enquiry and learning. Much will depend upon the creativity of individual learners, or the degree of openness and trust they have in the process, or their motivation and commitment to learning. It is obvious that personal values will play an important part in the fruitfulness of holistic educational approaches, and that therefore education in values cannot be left to chance or treated as insignificant. Personal, social and moral education are therefore part of the core of learning. The emphasis upon an experiential and reflective approach also implies that the curriculum should deal with issues that are controversial, that is, which are unresolved in everyday life. Social, racial and sexual prejudices cannot be denied attention, and the curriculum must acknowledge some at least of the political, cultural and ethical issues that divide society.

The holistic perspective offers new criteria and prompts new questions: What happens to the curriculum if the subjective is taken into account? How do we build a curriculum around immediate awareness and experience? How can the elements of non-cognitive discovery, the affective, the physical, the tacit, the intuitive, be incorporated, and should they be? The holistic argument is that a model of the curriculum that recognized the human being as body and spirit, as well as mind, would be truer and more complete than the detached understanding in which knowledge is seen as independent of the knower. And thus many writers and educators have searched for a holistic approach to education in which all these elements had their contribution and their place. The common criticism made was of the way learning was structured into separate and parallel subject tracks covering previously determined content. However convenient for teaching purposes, this falsified the nature of knowledge, which cannot be understood as either fragmented or static. The tendency of thinking always to relate itself to a fresh idea, the inadequacy of any assumption that we can be detached observers entirely separate from what we are thinking about, the failure to acknowledge that while being logical we also function psychologically, while thinking of the individual we need also to think of the social, and while thinking of the scientific we must also have in mind the cultural, were reservations that have been increasingly widely shared, despite current official policy-making trends in many western societies.

The issue is caught by the passage from Hofstadter's *Prelude...Ant Fugue* at the beginning of the chapter. In the ensuing dialogue, pursuing the nature of the holistic, Anteater sees the ant colony as subject to exactly comparable though dissimilar external pressures to an individual ant. He rejects systemic views and teleological interpretations. There is even an indirect reference to the brain hemisphere theory, in which the right brain is associated with the holistic view (Hofstadter, 1982: 163ff.). It is not only biology that engages in this debate, however; it is all the subjects of the school curriculum and, of course, theorists of the whole curriculum. For example, in physics, there is the issue of the interaction of the observer and the observed, which suggests the need to take things at a higher level of analysis such as the implicate order proposed by Bohm. In economics, the new concern for alternatives to growth stems from a broader ecological consciousness. In art, there is the idea of the hidden order which brings things into relationship, for example in the 'intelligence of feeling' (Witkin, 1974). In sociology, the intersubjective process of the social construction of reality demands an interdisciplinary focus (Berger and Luckmann, 1967). In technology it is the need to take the global view of the problem to be solved within both its scientific and social context.

A different perspective is obtained by considering the work of Illich, whose demand for de-schooling was seen as the need for society to move away from manipulative towards convivial institutions (Illich, 1971: 53). The impact of this upon the curriculum was to subordinate it to the interests and needs of learners. One way of generating this kind of learner-centred curriculum was Freire's approach through 'generative themes'. The idea is well illustrated by an incident recounted by Illich:

> I have frequently witnessed how discussants grow in social awareness and how they are impelled to take political action as fast as they learn to read. They seem to take reality into their hands as they write it down...and I remember another (man) who on his way to work stopped with his companions and wrote the word they were discussing with his hoe on the ground: 'agua'.
>
> (Illich, 1971: 18)

Freire's notion of 'humanization' is holistic in character, as is the process of conscientization, or critical awareness leading to praxis, in which action and reflection are combined (Freire, 1985, chap. 7). Knowledge is generated by the interaction of a person and their environment. When Roszak refers to person and planet having similar needs he foresees this interaction, but Freire finds it in what he regards as the fundamental educational processes of dialogue and co-intentional pedagogy. Bohm's concepts of the implicate and explicate orders seem to me to be powerful ideas for holistic education, but I have not seen them explored. He does refer to what he calls 'experience–knowledge' (Bohm, 1981: 6), so that one can infer that the knowledge to be sought is, as it were, enfolded in experience, perhaps even dormant in earlier experiences, waiting to be evoked. This is not a new idea in education, of course, but there are interesting new dimensions to the subject that could be extended from the scientific applications of the theory that Bohm has set out.

Many such insights are far from having been incorporated into conventional education, and in fact many educational innovators have had to establish their own schools to have the opportunity of practising the form of education in which they believed. Bertrand Russell and A.S. Neill are well-known examples of this; so also is Rudolph Steiner, whose notions of 'the ultimate unity of human experience' and of the 'metamorphosis' involved in education were characteristic of holistic insights that inspired a whole system of new schools. In his appraisal of Steiner's work, Harwood emphasizes how Steiner recognized that 'the whole human body, and not the brain alone, is a vehicle of consciousness' (Harwood, 1958: 20). This notion stimulated work on body rhythms and links between body, mind and feelings that has been virtually ignored in conventional education. There thus exists an enormous field of work to be explored and brought into relation with curriculum design, because of the tension between the rational approach, with its fragmented, intellectualized knowledge, and the holistic view, with its requirement for a curriculum that is integrated, centred on the person in body, mind and feelings, and experiential.

What I believe to have been forgotten in this shifting and crystallizing of positions is the nature of the cultural background from which western society and education originally came. The pre-scientific holistic view of life and education that characterized Europe from early Benedictine monastic times was the source of western civilization, of both its rational and moral or spiritual elements. In fact, these origins have not only been forgotten, they have been repressed, to the extent that it is now almost impossible to speak of a moral or spiritual heritage, especially the latter, without a quiver of trauma – so profound is the taboo. My own conviction, to be explored in the following chapter, is that we need to return to the spiritual, which I see as concerned with the ultimate ground of our being, the opening to meanings and purposes for our existence that are not created by humanity, but are given in our very natures by a higher power, whether we wish or not to acknowledge this power as God.

But the practical implications of a holistic viewpoint for education, whether or not it includes a spiritual dimension, are very far-reaching, and I believe of crucial significance. The training of the intellect in rational procedures can only be a small part of the education of the whole person. Rational education imposes what is known and the ways of acquiring and generating such knowledge, while holistic education must respond to the needs and wants of learners. A well known example of this tendency in holistic education is the model proposed by Carl Rogers. Rogers speaks of individuals having 'a directional tendency towards wholeness' (Rogers, 1978: 240), or 'a trustworthy function of the whole organism rather than of some portion of it' (Rogers, 1978: 243). His judgement of contemporary education was that 'individuals are culturally conditioned, rewarded, reinforced for behaviours that are in fact perversions of the natural directions of the unitary actualizing tendency'(Rogers, 1978: 247).

Most of the work Rogers did in education, for example as reported in *Freedom to Learn for the 80s* (Rogers, 1983) and *Carl Rogers on Personal Power* (Rogers, 1978), was through adult self-directing groups. However, he formed part of, and indeed led, a whole movement of therapeutic action with valuable implications for school-age education. The emergence in the 1960s and 1970s of such humanistic disciplines as personal counselling, Gestalt therapy, encounter groups, psychosynthesis, group dynamics, co-counselling, transactional analysis, bio-energetics, acupressure, and many other techniques, was part of the recognition of the human being as mind, body and spirit in therapy and in education. Some aspects of these therapies have since been absorbed into teaching and counselling in education, and are now playing an increasing part in the training of teachers, particularly in post-experience courses. What might be claimed to be a further stage of such work was reached with the development of more elaborate approaches to human transformation, such as the *est* training in the West, and transcendental meditation or Zen as imported disciplines from the East. The appearance of new religious movements, such as Scientology and the Reunification Church perhaps represented even a different option, where conversion of life into a specific community was demanded. The educational, or possibly conditioning, impact of these approaches was powerful wherever it reached, but it was not generalized, and in fact is likely to be strongly resisted in schools.

Recalling the five propositions offered in Chapter one, it is clear that holistic approaches in education place individuals firmly in the position of being responsible for self and, collectively, for actions undertaken in society. There is a presupposition in favour of equality of persons, regardless of such distinctions as can be rationally made between sexes, races or social groups. The fulfilment of individuals also requires opportunities for self-determination, the development of talents and potentials, and participation, as well as the enjoyment of positive relationships. And, perhaps above all, the right to develop a personal perspective on the world and a moral vision.

Such thinking tends to encourage a more inclusive approach, not only to the human person as body, mind and spirit, but to social institutions, to human society as a whole, and to its ecological and even cosmic context. We can therefore identify a continuum of contexts for holistic education leading from the basic level of the whole person, which is already beyond the scope available to pragmatic and rational approaches to education, and rising through successive steps to the teacher–pupil relationship, the community of the school in its epistemological, cultural and social dimensions, the wider human community and the context of the human race as a whole. It can be said that each of these levels is relevant to an authentic education. Just as a peaceful world is impossible to attain when positive affectivity is denied in the curriculum of schools through coercive teacher–pupil relationships, so authentic education is impossible in a society that collectively denies human rights.

The implications of such holistic thinking for the kinds of educational institutions needed, the characteristics, qualities and skills of the teachers, the nature of pedagogical relationships, the structuring of learning experiences, the style of linkage between schools and the wider community, are all themes which educators are currently exploring within state systems of education to some degree, but mainly through alternative schools. In theory, such work offers a massively important alternative to pragmatic and rational education, but in practice it remains a minority pursuit, even a cult. Thus, far from absorbing the rational into a broader context, the holistic has become increasingly polarized in relation to what is the politically dominant model of education in modern western society. Instead of resolving the social crisis, holistic thinking in education risks becoming polemical, accusatory, politically marginalized or alienated, sectarian and self-righteous. The 'reason' for this is simple enough to appreciate. There is no holistic orthodoxy or consensus; there are merely widely discrepant and therefore competitive variants of the basic insight. How can we stay with the basic insight of the holistic securely enough to acknowledge and indeed celebrate our rational capabilities? This is a question that refers us to the spiritual domain.

Holistic thinking and the spiritual

The holistic movement in modern thinking has been as much one of lifestyle as of thought through philosophy. There is a certain fusion of values, which many would call either holistic or spiritual, and which is represented in Figure 1 as category E. It would, for example, be hard to deny that, within the last generation, the colour, freshness and courage of the hippies, the Peace Corps, and similar voluntary and cooperative movements, especially in the ecological field, have brought about certain profound and irreversible changes in western society. To pretend that prosperity was evil while benefiting from all the freedom and the ease of travel that it bestowed might be judged a superficial attitude, but this was only a first stage. We are too near these events to understand exactly what happened, but a greater integrity and integration developed in the civil rights movement, in anti-war protest, in student struggles for individual freedom and political participation, in concern for the Third World, in the flourishing of social sciences as an effort to confront world problems, and in the blossoming of new philosophical and spiritual movements that sought to propose a holistic way forward out of the rational–scientific morass.

Among such movements it has been impressive to see the headway made by the Greens in recent years. Their thinking has been progressively adopted by conventional political groups, and its spiritual potential is suggested in a challenging way in the *Brundtland Report* with the proposal that:

> The world's religions could help provide direction and motivation in forming new values that would stress individual and joint responsibility towards the environment and towards nurturing harmony between humanity and environment.
>
> (World Commission on Environment and Development, 1987: 111)

What remains to ponder is whether in the world of conceptual polarities, the mechanistic and the organic, the cognitive and the intuitive, the didactic and the experiential, there can ever be a resolution. In his philosophy of education lectures at the University of Chicago, Joseph Schwab used to speak of the 'lumpers' and 'splitters', that is the Platonists who saw things as a whole and the Aristotelians who subjected aspects of the material and mental worlds to analysis. Are we going to be like Anteater, who declares himself ready to change his perspective when it suits him (Hofstadter, 1982: 174), so that we corruptly take a pragmatic view of the rational and the holistic, or can we find a genuine synthesis between the two basic perspectives?

To answer this question requires us to take a further step in our explorations. The spiritual can be approached as the context within which human thinking and feeling can be synthesized, in which they can both find their fulfilment. Will we then find that the spark of genuinely transcendent spiritual insight is still alive in the depths of the secular city, even if masked by rational or holistic theories with their assumptions either of probabilism or of truth that is immanent, that is, valid only for a particular time, place or situation?

Note

1   Dr Ted Cantrell, at a Conference on Holistic Models of Man: Educational and Medical Perspectives Compared, Southampton University, 27 September 1986. The Conference was one of a series on 'Spiritual Values and Education' which has been running since 1984, and which is further referred to in Chapter seven.

The transcendent perspective

At a voice workshop, Derrick sang a song he had written himself,
a plaintive, self-revealing, suffering song. A few years later at a
chance encounter he was asked if he had written any more songs.
'No,' he said, 'I'm spiritually dead.'

Song-writing seemed to Derrick to be a spiritual pursuit. The quest for
the spiritual, whether Derrick's or our own, is certainly not an
intellectual one, but to write about the quest is to run the risk of being
trapped into defining and limiting a reality that is wholly other (Otto,
1923). The alternative is to see the search as a sharing, in which being
tolerant of other people's ideas and responses makes effective our
openness in our own search. Without an open, experiential and reflexive
stance that mirrors the integrity but not the methods of the scientist, the
project of a search for the spiritual must be abortive. There is no easy
answer to Derrick, except the enigmatic one of the need to be ready for
the unexpected. And the search must be lifelong.

An experiential approach to the spiritual

It might be a contentious matter to speculate to what extent education is
'spiritually dead', but there is little doubt that the pragmatic instinct
offers the most profoundly unsatisfactory basis for taking educational
decisions. Scientific rationalism and holistic approaches, as the previous
two chapters have shown, bring many more considerations to bear, but
the object of this chapter is to explore virtually an alternative to the
pragmatic, one which is different from either the rational scientific or
the holistic. The aim is not to argue for an exclusive mode of thinking,
but to ensure that, in considering rational and holistic contributions to
educational policy, the claims of the spiritual are not forgotten or
underestimated as has tended almost universally to be the case. This
chapter takes the view that the recognition of the human being as having
a spiritual nature carries radical implications for life as a whole, and thus

also for education. This view will be put uncompromisingly so that it can be appraised clearly and straightforwardly. It is not being suggested that humanity is *only* spiritual, though the immediate intention is to consider the perspectives characteristic of category C of Figure 1. The view of education therefore that emerges at this stage is a necessary corrective but still insufficient or incomplete exploration. The further question remains: even assuming with Jung that modern man is 'in search of his soul', can he then reconcile his everyday personal, social and professional life with a spiritual conviction (Jung, 1933)? Are they two separate things, or can there be a synthesis?

The Enlightenment was man's challenge to whatever powers or forces might exist independently of him. For this reason the issue to be decided is a definitive one. Either this project is valid, and the world will be transformed in a way from which there is no return, or it will prove to have been what Christians see as the repetition on a large scale of the immemorial rebellion of humanity against its Creator. According to the latter view, it is not possible to conflate liberal rationalism and a spiritual understanding of reality. The spiritual transcends the rational, but cannot reveal itself to the rational intelligence. The spiritual can only be 'known' by the spirit, not by the mind. But the intellectual West rejected the spiritual and the theological precisely because these claimed other sources of knowing than the rational. It would be surprising if it were to accept them again now, or even to grant them more than a residual tolerance.

On the other hand, individual persons can look at things in a more integrated way. Many writers and educators of the kinds referred to in Chapter four have accepted a holistic view of education in which the whole range of experience of the human being, mind, heart and body, individually and in community, had their contribution and their value, even though there has not been a cultural transition to a holistic, still less to a spiritual consensus. Thus, while keeping options open or enjoying the aesthetic, creative and intuitive aspects of reality remain a possibility for those who take a broad view of the spiritual, the more that people have explored such holistic alternatives, the more polarized the resulting viewpoints have become.

I believe that the spiritual can transcend this polarity. As Tresmontant suggests, there are three metaphysics available to us: that reality is an empirical fact known to us by our senses; that reality is an illusion and exists only in our consciousness; and that reality is a creation of God which we can come to know by the measure in which we accept to be open to it (Tresmontant, 1980). These three positions correspond to the rational, holistic and spiritual alternatives that are being explored in this work. The implication is not that our rational powers are unavailing, or that our imaginations are misled, but that we need always to leave space for the whole scope of our awareness, rational, holistic and spiritual, in all aspects of existence.

An empirical approach to studying personal experience of the spiritual is feasible, and substantial relevant social survey work has been reported by the Alister Hardy Research Centre at Oxford (Hardy, 1979; Hay, 1987). On the other hand, every reader can be regarded as a subject in such a study, or can carry out the study for themselves. There are ways that our experience can take us beyond the rational and the holistic towards the spiritual. One possibility is by introspection, for example by taking an experience of suffering and, instead of concentrating on its immediate impact, recognizing that there is a limit to such experience in death. The notion of death as a releasing process may summon up a state of peace that can relativize the suffering encountered. Such moments of insight have seemed to many of those studied in Hardy's and Hay's research, and elsewhere, to transcend the purely psychological, and indeed are frequently described in histories of religious conversion.

Another approach to the spiritual can be found in turning towards others, but with an awareness that goes far beyond the immediate experience to the universal. This might lead to experiencing the self in the other, or to feeling prompted to recognize a person or their behaviour as a sign of truth, or as a reminder of one's own longing for integrity. And, thirdly, one can direct awareness to a transcendent power or presence, to which some people find they can feel united by sharing without any loss of identity, and which represents the deepest level of meaning and destiny.[1] This last position is meaningful from many different religious perspectives, and is, for example, epitomized for Christians by the sense of the unique character of Jesus as the one who is identified with the Absolute and is able to reconcile God and humanity. While I do not contend that evoking the spiritual by these means is necessarily meaningful to every reader, I do hope the point can be taken that an experiential progression into spiritual understandings, values and beliefs can be viewed as an essential element of human existence and our reflection upon it.

Extending the definition of the spiritual

Personal insights into the spiritual are obviously valid for individuals and useful for personal decisions in life, but they do not necessarily help another person. On the other hand, there is no way that we can satisfactorily conceptualize the spiritual and explain it in a manner that will command assent as in a logical discourse. Thus, the word spiritual is used widely but rarely defined other than with the greatest tentativeness. It occurs in the 1944 Education Act, and again in the 1988 Education Reform Act, though without definition. But can we continue to take the term for granted, as if we all agreed on its meaning? The approach I have so far employed in this work is to suggest a broad definition of the spiritual as the source of ultimate meaning, purpose and direction in life. At this point, and before considering what relevance the spiritual might have for education, I need to explore more fully the possible scope of the spiritual, and the associated notions of values and belief.

A number of points that can be made about the spiritual may attract a fairly wide measure of agreement.

(a) It has several times been suggested that the spiritual extends beyond rational and sensory forms of knowledge. It is not anti-rational, but has its own dimension of awareness, and cannot be reduced to psychological or social facts. Thus to speak of the spiritual poses problems of language and evidence. We may know more than we can express. Spiritual intuitions are formless, though they may still refer to a reality with features much sharper than the ones known through reason or the senses. Such intuitions wax and wane in an unaccountable fashion. It is not always possible to hold onto them. There are moments, in encounters with others and in experiences of life, and in times of reflection, when we may feel that we are not deceived. But these are intimations that it is often impossible to communicate adequately.

(b) Unlike the rational, but not the sensory, what we know of the spiritual is unique to each person. It corresponds to our inner self, perhaps to an inner voice or conscience, and it demands of us a response of integrity and commitment. If there is a 'proof' of the existence of a spiritual domain it lies in our own deeply-rooted care for finding the real and the genuine in such areas as our personal lives, relationships and work. For example, does it not make us sad that we are missing the mark in truthfulness, that we are not able to be frank or to sustain the position we have taken up because we want two things at once: the truth and the advantages of deceit, ambiguity or pretence? When we know that we are travelling in the 'wrong' direction it saps our energy for good. It would be naive to maintain that completeness is easily found, but disingenuous to claim that there is never an inner voice chiding us for our self-interest, for blocking our ears, covering our eyes, distracting ourselves with everyday concerns so that we never choose what is needed to make a difference, to transform the way we live, to come into communion with the authentic by our openness and commitment.

(c) For the human being it is not possible to consider the spirit as apart from body, heart and mind, so that the notion is holistic, permeating our intelligence, our feelings and our experience. The argument for this has been developed in Chapter four, including the recognition that, for some, there is no essential distinction between the holistic and the spiritual.

(d) Though our perception of the spiritual is unique, what we are perceiving is universal, and it reveals without explaining the oneness of humanity and the world, and the value of existence. It allows us to sense the ultimate ground of our being, and thus how we belong to each other beyond all categories.

For many who could agree with what has so far been said there might be no need to go any further. This would sufficiently define their idea of the spiritual. Such was the case of the group of HM Inspectors, working on the school curriculum, who identified 'spiritual' as one of the eight adjectives describing broad areas of learning considered to be important for all pupils. Their definition was as follows:

> The spiritual area is concerned with the awareness a person has of those elements in existence and experience which may be defined in terms of inner feelings and beliefs; they affect the way people see themselves and throw light for them on the purpose and meaning of life itself. Often these feelings and beliefs lead people to claim to know God and to glimpse the transcendent; sometimes they represent that striving and longing for perfection which characterizes human beings but always they are concerned with matters at the heart and root of existence.
>
> (DES, 1977, Supplement)

This 'description', as it was called, was offered as a basis for further discussion. Its distinguishing feature, of course, is that it does not link the notion of the spiritual inevitably to the divine. This means that the category of spiritual suggested is available to a wide range of people, since even religious believers can feel their viewpoint is allowed for by the sentence commencing 'Often...'. Do we need then to make a strong point of connecting the spiritual to the divine if that is the way we understand the spiritual? My personal conviction is that we do. It has already been made clear that in this book the notion of the spiritual is being taken as implying the existence of God. Any other use of the term is ultimately reducible to a philosophical, psychological or sociological concept, tied to its own frame of reference, and the spiritual as a category becomes redundant. Such discussion of the spiritual is secular, or humanistic, since it makes humanity self-sufficient. It gives importance to the person, but only because the person is the locus of consciousness, not because the person is an entity related spiritually to the Creator. If there is no God there is no option about this, but if there is a God then we need a category of 'spiritual' that is reserved to what concerns the life that he shares with his creation.

It may have been considerations such as these that persuaded some of the members of the 11–16 Working Party on the eight adjectives to offer another description of the spiritual, one which reads:

> The spiritual area is concerned with everything in human knowledge or experience that is connected with or derives from a sense of God or Gods. Spiritual is a meaningless adjective for the atheist and of dubious use to the agnostic. Irrespective of personal belief or disbelief, an unaccountable number of people have believed and do believe in the spiritual aspects of human life, and therefore their actions, attitudes and interpretations of events have been influenced accordingly.
>
> (DES, 1977, Supplement)

This description is uncompromising in reserving the notion of spiritual to that which pertains to belief in God, and goes further than I would go in asserting what is effectively more definition than description. However, it does seem to me to be very important indeed that it should be possible to offer a view of the spiritual that depends upon a theistic belief, as in fact mine does. I therefore add two further extensions of my original broad definition:

(e) The spiritual represents a mode of access to a realm of being which is outside time and space but is not subjective. The spiritual reality is transcendental, and gives humanity a personal link to God, that is to the Absolute in goodness and truth, so that there is no conceivable human aspiration that can take us any further.

(f) The spiritual nature of humanity is not an option or something to be seen as an appendage; it is the *primary* identity that we have, and is more significant to our existence than any material consideration.

To speak of the spiritual as primary is to take a stand that is outside the categories of the human sciences and which owes nothing to them. In fact it is the other way around: because the spiritual is primary, we can come to a greater understanding of what it is to be human and to be a person by acknowledging the value of the 'material' in the perspective of the 'spiritual'. The unique identity of the person is even more strongly affirmed, since, however determining we see social forces to be in influencing character, each person retains ultimate responsibility for their own spiritual destiny and relationship with the ultimate source of being. The inner self is not God; it is only a reflection of God, just as the human body is not the personality, but simply its projection into the coordinates of time and space. My conviction, then, is that the spiritual thus conceived opens up horizons of hope for humanity, and that its implications for education are literally inexhaustible.

Values and beliefs

A commitment to the spiritual, I want to argue, implies a radical break with the status quo of scientific rationalism. It is the decision to step off the see-saw of polarized ideologies based on interests, and to accept such values as peace, love and reconciliation, freedom to serve rather than power, justice rather than might, wonder and reverence rather than scepticism, hope rather than the desire for control, as the reflection of a transcendent power, or God, possessing ultimate control over our destinies, and containing the source of meaning and value for humanity. In this latter view, spiritual values are absolute and, like religious faith, provide the context for life and work, and not vice versa. It is not a question of incorporating a spiritual dimension into our social commitment, but of having the intention of recognizing a spiritual dimension to every step in life. And this intention is not merely a conceptual exercise but an effort to direct the will in accordance with spiritual or religious inspiration. Such observance has a public as well as a private character. The sense in which we belong to each other both transcends the rational order, and demands of us a constant spiritual opening to others. What might it mean to speak of absolute values in this perspective? Truth, goodness, life, conscience, love, holiness, honesty – do these terms not become directions for living rather than legal boundaries that I need to steer within?

A major problem in discussing spiritual matters, as this text illustrates, is what language to use for the purpose. When we use everyday language to speak of the spiritual we may fail to communicate the essential, but if we go to a special language, such as that of religion, we may convey ideas other than those we intend, with negative results. Closely linked to any effort to evoke the spiritual is the imagination's use of metaphor, image, allegory, paradox, and other such indirect instruments. Absolutes can be spoken of only very tangentially, and thus there is no guarantee that any communication will be effectively understood. Someone who speaks of the spiritual cannot translate their insight into a complete logical argument, any more than can an artist or a poet.

Probably most will agree that the word 'values' is meaningful for the understanding of human behaviour, even if it is used only as a catch-all term for what appears to be motivating us. There is no answer to a convinced behaviourist. They have their faith to live by. But others will acknowledge that they can to some degree choose their patterns of behaviour, and have preferences about the ways they perceive the world and how they respond to it. At the most basic level we all have values, or we would not be able to put one foot in front of the other: why go this way rather than that? Most of our actions are the results of value assumptions rather than deliberate decisions. Grimmitt suggests that spiritual values, however, have a distinct nature: 'human spirituality is not merely a core value among others but the source of the human capacity "to value".' (Grimmitt, 1987: 128).

Our apprehending of the spiritual may be compared to this kind of experience. We can hold no external reality as certain, except by suspending disbelief. We are constantly a prey to doubts. It is always possible for me to lose the grip I normally have on sensory reality, and it is always open to me to take hold of spiritual reality. It is simply that the way I apprehend the spiritual is not like, for example, the way I plan my route from home to work in the morning. It is a movement of the whole being, feelings as much as intelligence, intuition as much as sensory evidence. Hervieu-Léger speaks of the Breton peasants who lost their faith as soon as they arrived in Paris, which she explains in terms of the loss of the rhythms of country life as well as the progressive privatization of religion (Hervieu-Léger, 1986: 38). This is a similar notion to the 'traditional plausibility structures' of which Berger and Newbigin speak (Newbigin, 1986: 13–14), but it occurs to me that even if it is possible to lose religious faith in this way, faith does not seem to be gained by increments of plausibility.

The ground upon which we hold values may be referred to as beliefs. Beliefs can of course refer to any significant area of experience, such as life or death, society, science, morality and so forth. If the spiritual is taken as implying belief in God as its ground, it is still the case that much of what is called religious belief is not necessarily spiritual at all. It can be simply the rationalized formulation of ideas. Theology need not involve the whole being. The religious belief in the spiritual is better referred to as faith, the knowledge possessed by the entire being that humanity is neither the sole nor the original possessor of consciousness. This faith–knowledge will not look like rational or scientific knowledge, because it cannot be expressed in terms that allow logical or empirical verification. But this in itself is no more extraordinary than the certain fact that I cannot prove I love my child. Whatever I do to try to prove it can never really indicate the truth of my love. I *know* that I love. Someone else can know that I do, out of their own experience and empathy without requiring a proof. Religious awareness which has sufficiently evolved as to be relatively consistent over time, and thus to be referred to as a faith, seems to me to have this same 'and that is that' quality about it. The rationalist may see a closed mind, but then so does the person of faith looking back at the rationalist.

86

We cannot, therefore, use the categories of rationality to advance our discussion of spiritual beliefs. For the rationalist, there can be nothing sacred, even if he can spin webs of ideas about the conceptual distinctions between the sacred and the profane (Newman, 1986). There can be no mysteries that are not invitations to deeper analysis, no powers that of their nature transcend human understanding. At the most there is the variable of time: before we have come to understand, and after. But the spiritual is not an intellectual frontier to be rolled back once and for all. Sometimes we see; sometimes we don't. And intelligence is little use as a guide. If there is a guide we can adopt it is probably virtue, and beyond that only the power of the spirit, or the Spirit.

It might seem that to state plainly, as do traditional believers, that they believe in a God who cannot be detected as existing by any method of proof, but about whom they claim to know through their trust in messages passed on by others, and through a faculty of their own consciousness which they call faith, is to invite being dismissed from serious discourse by the canons of contemporary secular culture. And yet in a sense their seriousness must be seen as of a higher level than that of even major scientists or philosophers who have rejected the idea of God. Such persons are concerned only with the conceivable ideas and actions that they can generate between now and death, and possibly everything that they are doing could bring more harm than good, and may be utterly fruitless. Why, in fact, do they attach significance to life? Their taking themselves seriously is, paradoxically enough, make-believe. They may be of significance to others, but they may not; and they will never know, at least not within their claimed frame of reference.

The hold over others who rely upon a faith in God exerted by traditional believers is simply that within their own frame of reference, they have everything they need to prove their value, and if one accepts their premises then one must also acknowledge that whatever truth there is, is correlated with human intellect, rationality or wisdom. Essentially, this describes the way the world is ordered, with the cautions against dismissing rational thought being very great. Why then is it possible to turn to faith? The notion of faith conjures up an alternative vision of reality, the field beyond the veil that separates the material and the spiritual. Faith involves knowing with the heart, that is, with commitment, with the will, rather than through theory or even practical awareness. The intellect cannot legitimately dismiss belief in the spiritual any more than the spiritual view can invalidate the rational.

We are speaking of two worlds which are complementary to each other, rather than contradictory. Intellectuals can believe. When they face the mysteries of life and death, of beauty and goodness, of meaning and purpose in existence, they cannot reduce them to scientific enquiries. They must believe, or they must simply look away. My contention is that the modern intellect too often looks away from the mysteries, and that this is not an authentic human stance. Morally, we must look at the mysteries and consider the possibility of faith in an explanation that transcends our consciousness. This cannot be done deliberately and systematically, but we can open our minds and hearts to the transcendent. Faith shows itself as a gift, not an inference. The intellect cannot produce faith. Just as some drawing exercises involve making an upsidedown sketch from a model in order to break the patterning imposed on the artist's mind by preconceptions, so we may get further with the spiritual if we begin with the will to believe, or *fides quaerens intellectum* as St Anselm has it.

Who, then, are those who claim to acknowledge the spiritual dimension of human experience? They are all those who 'know' that inner human nature overflows time and space. They may be members of groups holding elaborate religious creeds or viewpoints. They may be individuals who regard themselves as privileged possessors of illumination or divinely revealed knowledge. They may be people who claim to experience supernatural phenomena of healing, or visions and communications relating to an extra-sensory world. Or they may simply be those who equate the spiritual with what is most distinctively human in the natural world. We could look at a range of such conceptions. Some would be highly sectarian and exclusive, others would offer little that would not comfortably merge with the views of pagan poets or secular humanists.

It may be useful to distinguish the most other-worldly variants of the spiritual option in values. These are represented by the sects and cults, and indeed monastic and eremetical traditions, fundamentalists of Christian and non-Christian origins, and religious mystics, for all of whom the transcendental counts first and last. An element of this tendency enters into mass religion through such features as prayer and worship, pilgrimages, devotions, and the quest for holiness or enlightenment. However, it is not generally a feature of major religions, and certainly not of mainstream Christianity, to oppose spirit and matter as if they corresponded to good and evil. Usually, institutionalized religions have their own social and political projects in the world, if also their good works aimed at caring for those in need, or at bringing to others the faith and truths in which they believe. This reference to religious practice is important for the whole argument of this book, because it is evident from many sources that the more spiritually orientated religions are currently experiencing growth in the western world. Many of those social scientists who wrote of religious faith fading in the 1960s with the 'death of God' movement, for example, are now speaking of a return to religion. The American theologian Harvey

Cox specifically examines two contrasting types of new development, fundamentalism and liberation theology, and he concludes that they constitute part of a return of religion as a social force in the western world (Cox, 1984). Similar findings are reported for France (Hervieu-Léger, 1986), but it may be that such developments are less clearly discernible in Britain.

The spiritual dimension is thus recognized by many as their living link with the spiritual world. They do not find it strange that human beings should perceive a spiritual side to their natures; nor do they see the spiritual as something added on, but as an intrinsic part of experience. This 'knowledge' of the spiritual is shared by people of different faiths and philosophies through their beliefs, explanations, metaphors and traditions. The area of overlap or commonality of approach with other forms of thinking in science, the arts, health and religion is such that the old polarities, for example those of science and religion, seem to be breaking down. Is it not time to ask whether education should be taking account of sources of knowledge of humanity, and of the meanings we have for our lives, which arise beyond the scope of our intellects and senses?

Education and spiritual values

How much do educational theorizing and discussion raise questions of spiritual and religious belief outside the curriculum area of religious education, even in countries like Britain which require such teaching in state schools? RE may once have been thought an important subject for its effect on the behaviour of the young, but it is obviously not expected any longer to make any difference in this regard, if the time and resources devoted to it are taken as evidence. The thrust of RE in Britain, in the years following the 1944 Act, essentially responded to Christian influences. Social changes since the 1960s, however, have created pressures on most teachers of RE to adopt a multi-cultural and multi-faith approach, so that the subject has largely altered its identity to that of comparative religious studies within a predominantly relativist framework. That is, even RE has adopted a phenomenological methodology which conveys vicarious knowledge about religion and reflects the widespread view that faith is no part of education.

There is undoubtedly a need to look closely at the curriculum assumptions underlying not only RE but the culturally relativist perspective in so far as it has affected the teaching of moral and spiritual values. Watson has made a substantial contribution to this task (Watson, 1987), and so has Hill, writing in the Australian context (Hill, 1987). It is evident that people of all persuasions question themselves about spiritual values and beliefs, and about religion and God (Hay, 1987).

How can schools continue to treat these matters as irrelevant to education on the basis of an old-fashioned rationalism that no longer convinces, and no longer provides a basis for living or a reason for commitment in life? In a recent curriculum report from HM Inspectors, it was accepted that the spiritual can be 'understood only partially in rational or intellectual terms' (DES, 1985b: 32). Is it not time to search again in our spiritual natures for other insights and intuitions which can give us a firmer hope of supporting the young in finding answers to their most profound existential questions?

In seeking to characterize the spiritual dimension of education, it seemed helpful to distinguish 'timely' from 'timeless' values (Plunkett, 1985). Timely values are those concerned with immediate aims and pervading everyday life. At one extreme, such values are stereotyped and equate to crude self-interest, for example in highly segregated or selective educational systems exhibiting severe inequalities for different social groups, races or sexes. But there are timely values which reflect a greater degree of judgement, in which reason, tradition and experience have played a part, so that they can be offered as universal aspirations of human beings. Education thus draws beneficially upon timely values without needing to infer a spiritual dimension. For example, there is space in the school curriculum for concern with world peace, poverty and development, human rights and the protection of the environment. Teachers are, however, constantly constrained by a variety of pressures to balance every discussion, giving equal time to every viewpoint, and there is an attempt to bring about a morally neutral curriculum. The risk is then that particular value positions receive less emphasis than the skills of handling the debate between them. In so far as this happens, there will be no leadership or clear guidance for the young in areas of doubt, and no vision or goals for the institutions. A neutral curriculum is in fact a myth; either it affirms positive values or it affirms relativism or scepticism.

Timeless values are of a different kind. They reflect belief in an absolute, a truth that is not endlessly debatable, which is not the fruit of human intellect. Such values may result from reflection upon experience over a period of time or from a faith that appears self-justifying to individuals, or taken as authentic by communities of believers, for example in a church or a religious faith. The spiritual is precisely this quality of timeless wholeness, or holiness, that stems from opening to the absolute. This takes us beyond reason, beyond the sensory, beyond common sense, which all bid us to accept that we are circumscribed by time, space, and strict limits on our physical and mental processes. Yet we are also prompted by a sense that we are capable of making more of our lives and our world than anyone has yet seen. We are drawn to work for justice, peace and welfare on a world scale, and that influence acts on us in our own awareness and imagination. The spiritual thus reconciles reason and conscience in a particular and individual awareness. It is not a cultural form, however much it may have cultural or timely manifestations.

To apply a spiritual perspective to education means accepting to see it other than in the light of the timely. This is to take another direction from the essentially pessimistic view of man and of education followed by so many ideological currents of the present time. The timeless, spiritual view of humanity is fundamentally an optimistic one. The problems and evils of our time will yield. People are equally worthy of love and respect, and their intentions have meaning, even if no immediate answers are found to the questions that press us in time and space. There will be contradictions between the timeless and the timely interpretations of education; they imply different assumptions, different meanings to words, different values. This alternative view has been neglected, and this in spite of the fact that for many the spiritual dimension provides the principal source of hope for the future.

But how can we come to know the validity of any alternatives to western rationalism? We cannot simply abandon what we have and launch out anew without any criteria or preconceptions. The West is not about to unthink the positions it has arrived at over several centuries. The problem with such questions is that there is not going to be any rational answer to them. Any answers depend upon breaking out of the circles of western rationalism and pragmatism. This happened in the ancient world or is recorded in the Bible when prophets came and were heard. But who are the prophets today, and can they be heard? The most 'successful' prophets, among so many that were ignored, were those, like Moses, who had a message that related to what everyone saw was needed to avert a threatening situation, to reject a particular form of idolatry, to save a people from slavery. These words sound odd to the modern ear, but it is far from evident that they are not apt to describe the world we are living in today.

Many in the West are looking for sources of inspiration as ancient peoples looked to prophets, and all the more so because western societies and governments are virtually bankrupt of solutions to major world problems such as war and peace, hunger, Aids, poverty, race relations and the energy crisis. The modern fascination with eastern thought and religions is not solving these problems either, but it is provoking new reflection on the basic issues of the meaningfulness of our lives, and the possibility that they may have a purpose beyond our individual viewpoints. Despite these harbingers of a spiritual renewal, there is a sticking point in how little experience the West has of listening to anything other than its own history, or at least its own style of thinking. Where can we look to learn how to learn in new ways? Who will save us from our own cultural habits and traditions? Such are the immense tasks of education, far beyond the confines of rational and technological thinking.

In a work of the so-called 'new age' (Ferguson, 1982), the figure whom most activists in the various movements being studied had identified as inspirational was the Jesuit priest Pierre Teilhard de Chardin. In the latter's book, *The Future of Man*, there is a fifty year-old essay entitled 'Social heredity and progress: notes on the humano-Christian value of education'. It contains three points about the function of education in human society which deserve to be re-read today for their prophetic quality. In summary, de Chardin holds that:

> It is primarily through education that the hereditary biological process, which from the beginning has caused the world to rise to ever higher zones of consciousness, is furthered in a reflective form and in its social dimensions.
>
> (Teilhard de Chardin, 1982: 36)

Educators should honour 'the conquests of life' in their work, as:

> It is through education, by the progressive spread of common viewpoints and attitudes, that the slow convergence of minds and hearts is proceeding, without which there seems to be no outlet ahead of us for the impulse of life.
>
> (Teilhard de Chardin, 1982: 36)

And third, he affirms a christological understanding that the teacher, in transmitting both humanizing and divine influences, must see them as one, since:

> it is through the medium of education that there ensues... the gradual incorporation of the world in the Word Incarnate: indirectly, in the degree in which the heart of a collective mankind increasingly turned inward upon itself is made ready for this high transformation; directly, to the extent that the tide of grace historically released by Jesus Christ is propagated only by being borne on a living tradition.
>
> (Teilhard de Chardin, 1982: 37)

While the Christian language used may be unfamiliar to many, what is being portrayed is no narrow dogma, but the quintessentially spiritual function of education, as a 'living tradition', extending, raising and integrating human consciousness to its fullest extent, a movement which can be understood as true to human evolution in both natural and religious contexts. How then can such a function be realized?

The spiritual in educational practice

Although in Britain all religious education has the protection of law, the evolution of the subject in the school curriculum has been such as to eliminate its spiritual significance in very many schools. One of the reasons why the spiritual has so failed to evoke a response must be that it was tarred with the same brush as the rest of school knowledge, while suffering from a serious disadvantage. It was offered as a version of reality that represented adult opinion or experience at a time when this almost automatically invalidated it. But in fact the situation of the spiritual was worse than that of other areas of the curriculum, because while it is not considered indoctrination when the physics or geography teacher imposes knowledge or a style of thinking, it most clearly is taken as indoctrination when it is a question of imposed values and beliefs of a spiritual or religious character. If there is one thing that needs to be said about how education should approach the spiritual, it is that all learners need to be respected in their own experience of life, their own cultural values and patterns of life, their own spiritual insights and, above all, their own unfettered journey to commitment.

The problem the educator faces is how to reconcile the right of the learner to self-determination and the spiritual value of educating for conviction – not merely for opinion, as tends to be the case in western society. Is it indoctrination to break the taboo in education over belief and morality? There is undoubtedly a fear of belief and of absolutes, for these are commonly associated with fanaticism and rigidity in a society that has learnt to value pluralism and freedom. The contrary fear, however, is that teaching the facts matter more than opinions or values, that openness is an unqualified virtue, and that asking ever deeper questions does not imply any final answers, can easily become indoctrinatory. Between these two positions there must lie some ground where it can be agreed that, while all pressures on learners to accept ideas or pre-empting of their enquiries and manipulation of evidence is immoral, the sharing of convictions and exploring of other people's ideas, for example through the approach of 'critical affirmation' (Watson, 1987, chap.5), is essential if we want to avoid the trap of the neutral curriculum.

At the present time there is much concern about the lack of response of young people to religious education or to the spiritual aspects of life, and especially amongst adolescents who are exposed to such a cultural diet of materialism, media and even everyday violence, sexual incitation, alcohol and drug abuse, and socio-political marginalization. This situation surely makes the welfare of young people more threatened in the western world today than it can ever have been in any other society. In the capitalist world, the young are really at the point of greatest pressure, where secular materialism has bitten deepest, the most vulnerable and undoubtedly the weakest sector of our societies. It is not surprising that many young people have swallowed whole the values that society actually lives by, rather than any that are offered as a theoretical alternative in school. And this has happened even though these values, such as consumerism, the imperative of self-reliance, and the discarding of sexual taboos, work against them, and against them more than other age groups in the population.

To take just one of these areas as an example. I found in a study that I made of the literature that there was wide agreement in Western Europe on the need for more contact, dialogue, clarification of aims and the seeking of greater consensus between the various sectors and agencies concerned with the education and training of young people in preparation for work. I ventured to suggest that what was therefore needed was a coherent and flexible system of education and training that could reconcile needs for, amongst other things:

> an immediate occupation and lifestyle for young people leaving compulsory school;...engaging young people as participants in selecting and developing their own line of work and development;...staff development to ensure education and training methods which motivate young people and make the best use of the potential of those working in youth programmes; attention to the rights, needs and wants of the most disadvantaged groups, such as ethnic minorities, the handicapped, girls where they suffer from discrimination or stereotypes, and the many categories of socially inadequate young people who have become marginalised and alienated, for whatever reason; the balancing of the interests of employers in industry and of young people seeking to join the labour market.
>
> (Plunkett, 1986b: 29)

From a spiritual perspective these arguments are even stronger. In fact, it can easily be seen from this that spiritual values do have unavoidable socio-political implications. If it is a question of restoring the person to the centre of educational concerns, no spiritual significance is necessarily implied, since a humanist could claim as much. But the scene is set for going further. There is a gulf between spiritual and materialist perspectives measured by the tension, or even the contradiction between personal and social claims. The person-centred view that spiritual values enjoin, transforms our understanding of education as concerned with reconciling and meeting the needs, rights and wants of learners, and thus denies the state or the economy ultimate rights over the person.

In the circumstances it is not improbable that the young will be swifter than their elders to realise that a world built upon the materialist values of western society cannot survive. This awareness is growing, but the urgent need is for an approach to educating that accepts and develops the capacity of young people for spiritual regeneration. In *The Original Vision*, Robinson includes a chapter which details his subjects' disillusionment with their schooling in a spiritual perspective. One forty-three year old woman recalls:

> Schooling, teachers, books and general environment seemed in a completely separate compartment from my development of religious awareness .... I deliberately inhibited the inner life and became highly scientific in outlook, questioning my 'hunches' at every turn, and learning to be silent about them. I would willingly have talked of the inner life, if the setting had seemed right; but it wasn't, and this didn't much concern me. I enjoyed school and learning very much.
>
> (Robinson, 1975: 86)

These recollections, presumably of around the 1950s might be thought to bear little relation to contemporary conditions, but recent research by the Alister Hardy Research Centre has uncovered the high proportion of young people who admit to experiences that they would regard as spiritual or religious, far in excess of any proportions who belong to churches (Robinson and Jackson, 1987). When the huge sample of 6,000 sixteen-to-nineteen year olds who were included in the survey were questioned about which subjects in the curriculum had most spiritual impact on them, a large minority responded 'none'. There is a dimension of life that is being neither tapped nor cultivated by the modern curriculum. Is it unrealistic to think that it could be? Or irrelevant to think that it should be?

The Research Centre is now attempting to devise new teaching approaches which are different from most of the work attempted over the years in religious education courses. The keynote of the work is that it is experiential. That is, it encourages experience, directly or through exercises and simulations, and leaves time and appropriate opportunities for reflection upon experience. For example, there are exercises in meditation, in self-awareness through breathing, silence and reflection upon feelings (Jones, 1986). Exercises developing upon such a basis are now being introduced by teachers into their classrooms. These include work on developing personal insight and empathy for others, whether friends or people in contrasting circumstances, who may be experiencing suffering, tragedy or severe need. The most original aspect of this in the modern curriculum is the introduction of self-imposed disciplines of silence and meditation in the classroom, but such methods tend normally to be introduced only by teachers who have recognized a spiritual need in themselves.

This situation therefore challenges the teachers first and foremost, since in present social circumstances, apart from parents who more often than not feel uncertain or helpless, it is only teachers who have contact with the young at a time when they are most at risk of absorbing the values of society uncritically. How can teachers respond? It must be the case that teachers need first to look into themselves, to consider their own beliefs and values afresh. In a world where there is famine, poverty, war, corruption and waste, and where all of these things are tolerated, indeed abetted, by the western way of life, teachers cannot expect to be heard as sincere if they are seen by the young to be defending or colluding with the way things are.

It is my experience that there are teachers who see these issues in spiritual terms, and are beginning to look for ways to explore this dimension and break the spiritual taboo. But how are they to embark upon the nurturing of spiritual values in the schools? One answer to this must lie in their pursuing the spiritual values that lead them to forms of dialogue and experiential sharing that have been discovered to be most effective in other forms of educating. A saying has it that when we approach another person we are on holy ground. We cannot ride roughshod over their view of the world and their sensibilities. We have to acknowledge others as persons, listen to their voices, however faint in expression, and seek to understand how they interpret the reality they are living. This must be true whether the other is nine years old or ninety-five. But how does this approach lead us to the spiritual? The spiritual expresses itself fundamentally in the quality of relationships, in the strength of concern and love, in sensitivity for the uniqueness of the other, in the value given to persons, and in the justification attached to such attitudes. Only gradually will teachers have the opportunity to explain the whys and wherefores of our position, but they will have established the basis for that explanation by the consistency of their respect for others, regardless of their age or status.

The spiritual as curriculum

There are some challenging organizational as well as epistemological questions to be faced if we are to see better what place the spiritual can come to occupy in the school curriculum. How, for example, is it possible to have large numbers of adolescents in total silence in the classroom reflecting upon their lives and feelings? Which subject will it be, and how will this be justified to the young people themselves and to their parents? Almost by definition, people can only be initiated into such procedures by those who have themselves benefited, and who understand what is going on. A report on work of this kind in a mixed comprehensive school suggests that the potential interest of young people in practical approaches to spirituality in the classroom may have been very much underestimated (Beesley, 1988).

Moreover, the challenge to justify experiential methods in the spiritual area is one that is not being directed at traditional school subjects, many of which might be hard put to defend their content and methods if it were, and especially those which are most loaded down with what are called 'facts'. The curriculum needed is one in which many areas that are currently treated as optional need to be accorded priority. This does not imply new subjects necessarily, but it would mean a new approach permeating teaching, particularly by building upon current practice in process-based curricula.

The curriculum of religious schools

It is worth considering whether Christian schools, or indeed Jewish or Islamic schools, have found approaches to the spiritual which could be relevant to curriculum development in secular schools. Christians have always believed in and been optimists about education, understood as a complete process of personal development in which the intellectual aspect cannot be accorded pre-emptive rights. They have paid to support it, often over and above normal taxes. The Chapter one propositions might well attract support in Christian education circles, but it might be assumed that they referred largely to secular society and schools, not to church schools. Here it would be possible to argue a whole new programme which is largely neglected by the Christian schools, at least those of the major denominations in western societies (Hill, 1982). If Christian schools were really dedicated to spiritual values this would show up clearly in their curriculum, and it would be obvious to the wider society that the schools were equipping their students to enter it with a zeal for its betterment through their work, relationships and participation in its affairs.

Thus, what were called, in Chapter one, the 'pathologies' of society would be of central concern. If anyone has a moral obligation to espouse the causes of world justice and peace it is surely the self-confessed Christian. Given this, it is contradictory for Christian schools to be associated with elite education and to be unable to break out of the vicious circle of academic learning for its own sake, still less for the sake of personal qualifications and advancement of privilege. The fourth proposition is of no less concern to Christians in education. The old complacency of our educational systems, religious or secular, is gone. We are all obliged to face radical enquiry into how effectively we are addressing major human issues and commitments. Finally, it is even more contradictory where Christian education is mesmerized by the values of technological development and careerism rather than those of a person- and community-centred curriculum. The proposition that all people are equally worthy of love and respect, and capable of acting as reflectors of profound values, is surely synonymous with Christian ideals. If Christians claim that they see education primarily in spiritual terms this only gives them an extra dimension of responsibility, for there is no setting aside of the issues.

Why then is there not greater spiritual leadership from the Church in education? The resources of Christian education are enormous. The human resources of knowledge and experience are unrivalled. The worldwide contacts and exchange of ideas are such that Christian education should still be able to inspire as it has done so pre-eminently in past centuries. Even, and perhaps especially, in the most secular societies, where education has become locked in paralysing debate, the way out or forward, must involve the recovery of values that the Church has always struggled to hold. What would need to change for Christian education to make a serious contribution in the modern world is not its basic values, but rather its style, its readiness to dialogue with, and learn from the secular world, the enhancement of its own internal communications and the progressive development of its own educational programmes. In short, Christian education needs urgently to apply its spiritual principles to its own organization and development, so as to provide the inspirational strength to empower creative educational initiatives.

In curriculum terms, all schools have parallel responsibilities to those of Church schools. The only value in the modern world comparable to the spiritual forces that produced western civilization is the identification many wish to make with the interests of those who are economically, physically, morally and politically weak. This is not welfarism, however, since identification involves being of and with, not simply supplying, helping or ministering. Who can say that the nurturing of such values is not a task for education? Reporting its enquiries into the problems of inner cities in Britain, *Faith in the City* stated:

> We have been faced with the reality of alienation, poverty, powerlessness, a sense of failure and injustice, and a deepening polarization between the educational experiences of young people in urban priority areas compared with those growing up in 'comfortable Britain'.
>
> (Archbishop of Canterbury's Commission, 1985: 294)

It is very doubtful if any curriculum *content* can have an impact on such circumstances. Just as religious faith is not reducible to content, since it essentially represents a truth that has to be experienced more than grasped intellectually, so we need to find quite radical alternatives in the curriculum that enhance learning of spiritual values by direct experience, by human contact, by example of values lived, and by the testing of ideas and ideals in practice.

A curriculum open to the spiritual

Rather than looking for an entirely new curriculum, which might imply the judgement that all that has gone before was valueless or wrongly conceived, it appears that we need to review once more the creative curriculum work of recent years, in order to ensure that spiritual values are not stifled by its often overly rationalist aims. The fuller exploration of this topic is deferred to the final chapter, when it can be related to a broader theoretical context, but it is clear that experiential work in the curriculum can aim at something wider than liaison with industry, and health education can have a wider vision than assertiveness, or safe and happy sex. Left to themselves, numerous curriculum innovations in such areas as literature and the arts, personal and social education, or multi-cultural education, do very well to pick up issues that are tangential to the rational or utilitarian curriculum, but they tend to remain isolated and eventually run into the sand. Whole-curriculum thinking, demanded for so long by at least some curriculum theorists and social analysts, is really valid only if it includes the spiritual dimension. Rarely, however, is the spiritual mentioned in their texts.

The spiritual is set aside, either forgotten or relegated in favour of materialist concerns. We have only to look at the values underlying the most visible developments in education today to see that this is the case. There is no need to question the worthwhileness of such innovations as TVEI (the Technical and Vocational Education Initiative), information technology, education/industry liaison, graded testing, and so forth, but it is necessary to query the balance struck between them and such alternatives as the improvement of relationships in schools, social and moral development of young people, design and aesthetic considerations in school and community environments, the contribution of creativity and the arts to the quality of life and to personal sensitivity and development, education for peace and for a sense of the spiritual or religious depths found in history, literature and personal reflection. These latter concerns are being priced out of the curriculum.

The argument is continually being put that schools should be changing the curriculum to help meet the needs of society, to counter unemployment, and to increase wealth and social harmony or order. Just as often the argument is rejected, because it is said that education can only follow, and not lead society. The five propositions considered in Chapter one were all of a sociological or social psychological nature, even though they pointed to the central importance of values in society and to the vital contribution of education to the development of values. Now that the spiritual dimension of education has been extensively discussed, we can perhaps usefully add a sixth proposition, one which takes us outside the context of the 'timely', and which is concerned with the search for a framework or rudder for personal and educational regeneration:

Proposition 6: The spiritual perspective requires us to make educational judgements without reliance on rational or empirical evidence.

This proposition interacts with the other five. We have to judge by our insight into, or belief in criteria which do not come from existing political or other authorities, not even from our human reason. We know that this perspective consists in, according to a Russian Orthodox saying, 'placing our minds in our hearts'. This is not to be dismissed as blind faith. There is a human community that slowly and painfully builds its way in common reflection, perhaps most confidently within the tradition of religious thinking and prayer, but no less significantly by the mutual influence of all those who, in community life, politics, literature, the arts and sciences, keep their minds and hearts open to the ultimately valuable and the purposeful in our existence.

Consider the risks of the kind of curriculum, perhaps one like that which is officially favoured in Britain today, that becomes obsessed with acquainting children with the prowess of technological society. So many mechanisms of the modern world shield us from each other. Money is the main one. We buy privacy, time, space, leisure, the company of the people who suit us, who do not challenge us. We use our homes to hide in, and we watch the world outside with a wary eye through newspapers and TV. We use common services, such as power, transport and even the telephone, to increase our independence, to keep the world at arm's length. We become experts in knowing about things rather than being involved in them. For most, charity is achieved by telethons, fun-runs and the cheque-book rather than by direct personal care. There is less and less room in our homes for the handicapped, the elderly, the exploited. Lifestyle, hygiene, security-consciousness, ethnocentric stereotypes, and complacency are used to justify our own apartheid. Is there an alternative? Could we change enough for it to make a real difference? Could we be educated to see things differently? Are there ways of acclimatizing people to less fearful and repudiating approaches to each other? Is there a spiritual vision of the world and of education that can help us?

The answer to these questions cannot lie in a national curriculum, however many useful arguments are found for it. On the contrary it lies much more in the consciousness of individual teachers. There is a danger in their accepting that their jobs are increasingly defined for them rather than refined out of experience. If the meaning and value of a person's existence transcend the role given by society, then it is precisely in such a spiritual dimension that teachers can best find their vocation, as opposed to their job. How this might actually happen is further discussed in the final chapter, but the point needing emphasis is that in just the same way as teachers discover their own vocations they, in turn, are more able to recognize the vocations of their students. These too need to be enabled and empowered to decide to what they will commit their energies and their time. Society will not be worse off with committed and responsible members, but teachers must certainly struggle against the instrumentalist orientation in society that sees people merely in terms of their productive capacities.

None of this contradicts the usefulness of helping people to find ways to prepare for adult life and work, through skilled teaching and counselling, through new curricula such as pre-vocational programmes, or through direct links with the industrial world and similar innovations, but no innovation can enable schools to give students a meaning for their lives, and no school can justify ignoring students' decisions that stem from their uniqueness, their commitments and their conscience. If schools claimed otherwise, could they explain the existence of missionaries, monks, hermits, as well as hippies and drop-outs, or single mothers ready to die of hypothermia with their children? The crucial ingredient to the curriculum with a spiritual dimension is the constant struggle against the over-simplification of life by the application of materialist priorities and solutions. Indeed, rather than refuse curriculum change, it would be necessary for such spiritually attuned teachers to transform it into a process that honours the human person. This implies a more open, reflective style of pedagogy, by which learners are led to pose issues for themselves, and to answer questions as far as possible out of experience, insight and a growing awareness of the values they are choosing as a basis for their lives.

Thus, values and beliefs are not foreign to the content of the curriculum, but nor are they in any responsible notion of pedagogy to be handed down to learners. Since we cannot live humanly, as opposed to biologically, without valuing and believing, the task of the school is above all to ensure that opportunity is provided for the learning of commitment to personally chosen, yet never proven values. This is moral and spiritual education. We cannot maintain that morality is a private matter. It is rather the case that the teacher has his or her own moral responsibility to confront young people with issues of the kind that they in turn must face in their own lives. There are awkward professional problems to be faced. Where does moral education draw the line between experiential learning and discipline with regard to drugs? Where is the distinction between teaching and indoctrination in religious education? How 'situational' should the ethics be when dealing with Aids in schools? These are all issues where the outcome matters so hugely that the pedagogical problems must be rigorously faced.

These matters will not be taken further here, because we can embark on more detailed consideration of the implications of the spiritual for curriculum, pedagogy and school organization only in the context of a wider vision of education than has so far been proposed. The work of the next chapter will be to reflect on how we might arrive at that vision and what kind of character it might have. The concluding chapter then attempts to outline the kinds of educational tasks that would be entailed.

Note

1   These notions were largely theoretical for me until, in 1983, I read a newspaper article about reported apparitions of the Virgin Mary in Medjugorje, Yugoslavia. This is not the place to report the sequel, which I am hoping to do in *Queen of Prophets*, due to be published in 1990 by Darton, Longman and Todd, but it was life-changing for me as for many others. Of the twenty or so books available already in English on this subject, some frankly acknowledge the total implausibility of what is said to be occurring on any rational–scientific basis, but none the less show how the evidence is accumulating in conversions, healings and even scientific data on those claiming the visions (Craig, 1988; Joyeux and Laurentin, 1987).

Part three

Vision and task

Chapter six

The vision: education for mind, heart and spirit

The test of the whole argument and testimony of this book lies in whether the various perspectives on reality that have been explored in Part two can be synthesized so as to contribute to an education for mind, heart and spirit. The present chapter thus searches for a vision which can provide an understanding of the operating context for education, a vision that both reveals directions for choice and inspires with energy for action. The starting point for Part three is the book's thesis that education in western society today suffers essentially from a spiritual crisis. This stems from the fact that, as we have seen, notions of the spiritual contrast sharply. For some the spiritual does not exist, above all not as a transcendent power. For others the spiritual is merely an option in a world where we are free to choose our own way of seeing things. And for others again the spiritual is the primary reality, and reflects the existence of a Creator.

If I relate this to the situation of a reflecting individual, I find that even within myself I have constantly to clarify my own mind, to decide how I am to live, for what purposes, how I am to handle situations rationally or otherwise, and what action strategies I am going to use. But at the same time I am affected and changed by each passing moment, as new perspectives open up intellectually, emotionally, imaginatively and in other ways. I need the ability to respond rationally, organically and spiritually. Sometimes I have to react without being able to integrate something new into a rational view, but must allow for intuition, inspiration and feelings. For example, rationality may have to give way in deciding how to vote when I am influenced by certain key concerns rather than being able to take into account the whole range of possible issues. A full analysis evades me. I know that there are reason and emotion to persuade me in different directions. I know that not all rationality is good, especially if it comes out of a context of self-interest, and that not all emotion is good, especially if it is deaf to others' needs and concerns. Very clearly what we need in such situations is a more humanized rationality, or a more reasonable handling of feelings. The answer lies less in a decision between reason and emotion and more in a movement of integration. Any project needs this interplay of logic and intuitive feeling to be fruitful, but where do we stand to achieve the balanced approach? For this, a vision is essential, and it will be my contention that such a vision is fundamentally a spiritual resolution, at least in the sense that no resolution is possible without attention to the spiritual dimension.

It may have appeared from the foregoing chapters that the alternatives before us are so distinct as to be irreconcilable. If this were so we would simply have to make a choice. Are we satisfied, on the one hand, by an exclusively rational order? Or do we seek a holistic one? Or are we content with a purely spiritual view? It has, however, already been argued that these orders are incomplete without one another: that the rational needs the affective and experiential characteristics of the holistic; the holistic needs the meaning, purpose and direction offered by the spiritual; and the spiritual needs the grounding in time and space of the rational and the holistic. It is the nature of the vision to clarify basic assumptions about the various orders of reality and to define a total context as a setting for action. In terms of the argument of this book, therefore, it is the task of this chapter to explore the final area of the Map of the Values Terrain shown in Figure 1, that is, category G, defined by the overlap of the three basic circles of the rational, the holistic and the spiritual.

It will be clearer whether such a synthesis is feasible if we first examine the possibility that rational, holistic and spiritual alternatives are mutually contradictory, or at least contrasting, and that they have educational implications that cannot be reconciled. It is evident from the earlier chapters that the synthesis or overall vision that is being referred to is not without its problems, whether or not these turn out to be fundamental obstacles. The initial approach, therefore, will be to survey such difficulties, comparing the alternative perspectives with a view to clarifying their distinctiveness rather than, at this stage, their points of convergence.

Contradictions and contrasts

Mind, heart and spirit

The rational, the holistic and the spiritual faculties can be thought of as residing, respectively, in the mind, heart and spirit. But to what extent do these faculties form distinct categories, regardless of their functions or areas of concern? First, the mind might be said to deal with reality in terms of concepts which it creates by selecting that to which it wishes to pay attention. It accepts that reality is objectively knowable, though not yet entirely known, and that it can be known progressively and cumulatively only by being broken down into elements about which knowledge can be generated. There is a very significant educational prescription built into such a notion of reality. Given that our potential scope for knowing is so immense, we can aim in a school curriculum only to make judicious selections, to give illustrative opportunities for the use of the mind, in order to equip the learner to proceed autonomously thereafter. In a sense, therefore, the mind invents the particular reality to which it attends, though this may be done collectively, through 'intersubjectivity', as well as individually (Berger and Luckmann, 1967). The mind therefore invents rather than discovers meaning.

We take the heart in the sense not of a human organ but as a faculty for apprehending reality intuitively, directly, spontaneously and with feelings, exactly in the sense of Pascal's epigram that the heart has its reasons that reason does not know. We cannot ask if a poem is right. Its perspective on reality, if it is a genuine poem, is a personal truth, a truth of personal experience. It is not, in that sense, improvable upon by rational means. Its truth is subjective, that is, the reality to which it alludes is not separable from the perceiver, and it cannot be overridden by another truth, whether subjective or objective. Experiences aggregate both for the individual and through intersubjective sharing, so that they appear to extend the validity of the insights they convey, but they are always vulnerable to being cancelled out or transformed by strong emotional charges such as surprise, terror, love or shame. This arbitrariness of holistic awareness has simply to be accepted, as in the case of bereavement, even to the extent of requiring from us a total response of commitment, as when one's child is suddenly in danger, or perhaps is born seriously handicapped. The reality cannot be disputed; nor can it be fully dealt with by the mind.

In educational terms the implications are similarly fundamental. Schooling is not a substitute for living, and the psychological barriers between school and life must be broken down as effectively as possible to permit the learner to achieve his or her own unique view-point and understanding of reality. Likewise, the learner's conclusions must be respected by the teacher (Gattegno, 1970). In fact, the teacher cannot give the learner conclusions, but only structured experiences to enrich the process of enquiry (Dewey, 1963). Moreover, it is not possible to predict when a new insight will come from a major experience, or even if it will come, and therefore the pace of learning is also largely personal. This feature has been strongly supported by research into mastery learning (Block, 1971).

When we speak of the spirit we engage with an ultimate reality that we have no means of knowing other than through personal experience or, in the view of some, faith. This might be thought to entail that any spiritual knowledge would be unique to an individual, and yet there are spiritual beliefs that are shared by hundreds of millions of people. Spiritual belief or knowledge is none the less very difficult to discuss, and the truths of faith especially are not like the truths of reason or even of experience, which can be evaluated, on the one hand, by scientific procedures and, on the other, by observation, personal relationships, trial-and-error, and in a number of other ways. Spiritual truths remain unprovable, and yet people have constantly shown that they are willing to die for them. For data, then, we are left with the accounts people give of how they came to spiritual knowledge. Hardy argued that just as science could not deal with the nature of art but does not deny the reality of man's sense of beauty, so it must accept the reality of spiritual experiences, especially if they have been shown to follow patterns (Hardy, 1979: 4). The available modes of approach to spiritual knowledge are thus limited and specific. There is, for example, prayer, or meditation, where we can talk about methods and attitudes but can never be confident that we can communicate or share the experience with anyone else. Or there is access through other people who have received divine communications, and who are trusted as individuals, or as the representatives of a religious tradition or church to which commitment has been given.

Is it simply tautologous to speak of the spirit as being the site of the activity to which the spiritual refers? I do not think so, but admittedly we are in deep water. Leaving aside those who deny a spiritual reality, there are those who feel convinced that there is a spiritual level of experience in which we can all share, perhaps as we might all bathe in the same pool – but with the significant difference, if we can imagine it, that the pool only comes into existence as we bathe. In other words, we produce the spiritual out of our sharing. However, for those who see the spiritual as the fundamental reality, the context within which physical and mental reality exist, it is possible to postulate a spirit as an individual context for a personality and mind. This is, in my understanding, a way of formulating the traditional Christian doctrine of the soul. According to this view, each person is spirit and body and, in the spiritual realm, a person shares a level of existence with all other spirits. The spirit each of us has is thus unique, and belongs to a spiritual order of reality that is outside time and space.

How then do we draw educational conclusions from this? If we accept the authenticity of the spiritual, another's spirit and their spiritual experience are worthy of infinite respect. Any damage one does to another's processes of exploration of the spiritual denies one's own spiritual insight. However, as not everyone acknowledges the spiritual, it does happen that spiritual and religious enquiry and development are crushed in education, even banned altogether in many societies. This may be done in the name of reason, and this is the claim made in Marxist societies, but of course the consequence is that a spiritual option has actually been adopted: the option of excluding spiritual reality. The point is that neither option is value neutral.

Reason, intuition and faith

If we now look at the kinds of activity in which mind, heart and spirit engage, we could summarize them as reason, intuition and faith, respectively. Reason is one of human nature's most profoundly distinctive and useful assets. Existing in time and space, humanity has used the power of reason to establish its dominance over the planet, and to extend its enquiries into every corner of the physical universe. More than that, reason has been turned in upon itself so that we have acquired self-understanding and are now imagining possibilities of artificial intelligence, either in electronic or bio-genetic forms. Reason provides humanity with a means of defining, storing and accessing knowledge, while leaving to any eventual user the power to decide the purpose to which it is to be put.

Education, in this realm, is concerned with empowering learners to exploit the potentialities of reasoning in their own or others' interests, or to meet whatever needs or priorities they may have. Conventionally, the school curriculum tends to use familiar materials and settings to train learners in the powers of reasoning, beginning with simple procedures of memorizing, performing standard operations, following worked out examples of enquiries, treating problems isolated from context, but usually paying little explicit attention to the actual thinking processes involved. Usually it has been left to later stages of education to introduce notions of analysis, such as doubting, hypothesizing, inferring, verifying, generalizing, and so forth, and self-reflective aspects of reasoning have not played much part in conventional school education until the introduction of enquiry-based approaches, initially into science and modern mathematics curricula, within the past quarter of a century.

The strong conviction that learners could not be treated as isolated minds, when they had bodies, feelings and unique personalities, has led to many developments in education that could be said to transcend analytical reasoning by paying attention to intuitive and holistic forms of awareness. When the Chicago educationalists working with Bloom sought to work out a taxonomy of educational objectives, they worked with two major domains of learning which they referred to as the cognitive and the affective, and the work done to elaborate thinking with respect to the affective domain has influenced education irreversibly ever since. Valuing is seen as belonging to the affective domain, though this distinction was certainly overplayed. The key point is, however, that feelings, insights, intuitions, creative urges, and spontaneous expressivity are not to be thought of as random traits but as an essential part of human development, and something broader than rational thinking alone.

Another major feature of the intuitive and holistic is prescriptiveness, and the obligation it places upon us to accept experience. What is, is. If we are angry, envious, enthusiastic, or in love, then we are angry, envious, enthusiastic or in love. We do not have a choice. We can of course choose how to deal with, or even whether to deal with such feelings, but we have to recognize that they are there in us, or in the learner who seems unreceptive, bored, lazy or uncooperative. The cognitive approach to teaching gives us recipes for dealing with such situations, but without wanting to compromise its own objectives. The affective, or holistic, approach necessarily takes another line, such as: given the feeling-states and dominant experiences in the situation, what will lead on to greater personal development and enrichment, whether for the individual learner concerned or for the wider community?

The essential activity of the spirit is faith, in the sense that, without the constant act of consent to believe, the spiritual would effectively disappear from consciousness. The mystic indeed almost reverses this process by living as if absorbed into the sphere of the spiritual. Spiritual knowledge is direct, without an intermediary in time and space. Taking this as a radical statement of the spiritual, let us consider how it can be related to educational principles. Reason wants to treat as irrelevant anything that cannot be validated by sense data or by logic; the holistic vision accepts everything except obligation or constraint; and the spiritual implies deference to the power and initiative of the divine. This latter attitude is well understood in a Moslem, Catholic or Orthodox Jewish school, for example, where no proposition can be adopted in the curriculum that contradicts the truths accepted by faith. The value of the religious insight is absolute, though this is true only in principle, since not all practice will adhere. Thus, the contrary principles of the sceptical attitude of reasoning and the all-accepting openness of the holistic cannot be endorsed by a particular spiritual community as applying to its vision of the truth.

The empirical, ecological and transcendent

What distinctions are to be made at the level of the focus of concern of these three ways of viewing reality? Characteristically the rational sphere is guaranteed by its empirical foundations – though we have seen how some research scientists are beginning to outgrow this mould. If only what can be demonstrated to be real by sensory knowledge, or by scientific extensions of it, is real, then what counts as evidence is seen as objective, independent of the observer, and verifiable by a third party. Those areas of the school curriculum which share such features, that is mathematics and the sciences especially, are seen as particularly creditworthy and usually have the highest public status, both academically and in the job market. The curriculum follows general scientific practice in favouring specialization and the dividing up of reality into components that can, in terms of practical usefulness, be analytically distinguished for the purpose of both teaching and study.

This usefulness may not be so immediately apparent in the concern that seeks always to locate humanity in the widest context and to value the wider natural environment. Ecological thinking is not just the conservation of, but the caring for nature, a fellow feeling for organic life and for the whole planet, as Capra continually stresses (Capra, 1983, chapter 8). Evidence for a position held is not sought in rational terms but in strength of concern for and commitment to a cause or ideal. Phenomena are best understood when viewed as parts of a whole. Educationally, such principles have significant practical implications, leading as they do to multi-disciplinary enquiry, synthetic thinking, and a search for ways to combine arts and science perspectives.

The subject matter appropriate to the spiritual view-point is the transcendent, or the sphere associated with spiritual reality. Enlarging our vision to encompass all imaginable truth and goodness, and trusting in and hoping for union with a benevolent spiritual power, we come to be aware of and believe in that which transcends material reality. Learning therefore follows not from avoiding the question of God, but from attending to the divine in contemplation and in practical living. So we come to the central issue of whether it matters for education that we decide for or against belief in God. For the rationalist, God is unprovable, and therefore irrelevant to all educational intents and purposes. In rational terms, God is simply unknowable. In the holistic perspective, God can be envisaged as a possibility, an hypothesis, but there is no room for religious doctrines which could be in any way exclusive. From the spiritual perspective, God can be known as real through belief, though also through the testimony of others.

This issue matters vitally for education, because by acknowledging the spiritual dimension of education we inevitably raise questions about the ultimate purposes of educational activity. If there is no spiritual dimension to life, then only pragmatic and timely values are justified within a rationalist perspective, whilst the holistic view constitutes an open system, one able to accommodate whatever experience actually occurs. Once a spiritual dimension is affirmed, however, it is the spiritual that becomes the determining view. Either way, it is necessary to choose, but this does suggest the need to consider whether these view-points are as antagonistic to one another as has so far been inferred.

Areas of convergence

It is not the purpose of this section to contrive convergence or synthesis of rational, holistic and spiritual perspectives through an eclectic approach, still less by some encyclopaedic amalgam. As has been shown earlier, there are already compromises and accommodations between rational or holistic and spiritual view-points which lead to false solutions. We do not need more educational approaches which simply add to the existing aims of schools and further burden their curricula and timetables. The enabling question has to be: once we have identified an educational philosophy, what elements are needed practically to ensure that it can be put into effect? It will be argued here that rational, holistic and spiritual elements are all indispensable for contemporary education, and particularly within a context of social issues and concerns such as have been outlined in Chapter one.

Vision and task

In a world of time and space the spiritual insight cannot ignore the rational and the holistic. Any vision of education would, in this view, need to reflect the relationship of the ideal to sensory or empirical reality. The timeless, in other words, is seen as the context for the timely. The vision is necessary to action, because it provides the template and the energy to transform the timely reality. On the other hand, this reality reveals the immediate task in hand, the activity that forces itself upon us, that may be burdensome and confusing but which cannot be avoided. Vision and task need to be mutually aligned, though it often happens that the pragmatist forgets the vision or the other-worldly person forgets the task. The link between the two is not so obvious, for it depends upon insight, creativity, openness, personal conscience and, in the final analysis, surrender to the spiritual. Though the rational and the holistic provide indispensable starting-points, we cannot reconcile the timely and the timeless except through the spirit.

Rationality serves the spirit by, for example, organizing our existence in terms of tasks needing to be done, reminders of things forgotten or neglected, speculations about things unknown but which can be reflected upon, and by evaluating the results of past decisions. It is however too exclusively concerned with concrete results, such as, in education, the individual's performance or the measurable product of the investment in a school or course. This imposes upon the learner a requirement to satisfy the demands of the system, to submit to the standards of others, to downplay feelings and experience in favour of the objectively knowable, and thus to feel cut off from the self – while education itself is becoming cut off from everyday life.

The holistic serves the spirit by recognizing relationships between the unfamiliar and the familiar, by openness to experience, by risk-taking and challenge, and above all by seeking always to be inclusive and organic rather than exclusive and mechanistic. Rational remedies to current educational problems are insufficient in themselves. This is because the problems cannot be reduced to the material, to matters of resource use, people-processing, or the mere production and distribution of a commodity called knowledge. The holistic remedy in education is to start from the whole child, and thus greatly to multiply the needs and wants recognized by the educator. In fact, the functions of education rise to the potentially infinite precisely because of the openness of a holistic perspective to the total, and expanding, nature of the human material of education. The holistic approach has an impossible task in the real world of very large numbers of individual people, with the range of their needs, the variety of their cultures, and the competitiveness of their philosophies and ideologies. We currently see the struggle of the pragmatic rational and the holistic being fought out in Britain with the severe challenge of the enterprise culture, of having rather than being, which is being promoted by a strongly centralist government. Retreating into libertarian values of freedom for the individual, or into ideologies such as multi-culturalism or progressive sexual attitudes comes more and more to look like a new form of alienation.

The contribution that the spiritual makes to both rational and holistic tasks of education is to bring to bear a unique valuing perspective. It is not only the rational and the holistic that matter; it is not the case that everything is of equal value and that nothing needs to be constrained or to be fought against. Rational and holistic perspectives are limited in their insights. The spiritual power of discernment is essential to human nature; if we are denied its use we are only half human. Provided that the rights of an individual or group to its own spiritual enquiry and develop-ment are not interfered with, however, there is no essential contradiction between spiritual and other viewpoints as regards education for every-day life. Indeed, the insights of the spiritual view, and the commitment it generates, can support and enhance both rational and holistic educational principles, whether moral, psychological or social.

In its application to education, the spiritual perspective highlights purpose, and particularly final or ultimate purpose, and thus it offers the possibility of unifying purposes. This is only a possibility, of course, because in the context of time and space it is equally possible for the spiritual to be the occasion of division and conflict, as human history shows only too well. But this results from the needs and wants of the material rather than the spiritual nature of humanity. Another way of putting this is to say that the purpose of humanity, or of education, is ultimately spiritual, and it is only after this insight has been accepted that cultural and ideological conflicts can be resolved. How can we restrain the degree to which worldly possessions and political, racial or other interests matter? Is it not the spiritual quest of humanity to achieve this kind of enlightenment while inhabiting time and space? Is this not what the gospel and so many other religious traditions are telling us, even where, like Christianity, they see life as a journey which cannot be fully completed in this world?

Educational policy and the spiritual

Taking Chapter one's five propositions about the social context for educational policy-making as our starting-point, it may now be possible to indicate why it is being suggested that a new level of thinking that explicitly includes the spiritual is indispensable for finding a practical, and not merely theoretical response to society's crisis of values. If it is true that rising levels of aggression are undermining human relationships in western society, these are not problems that can be solved by force or by legislation. Relationships are areas of life that depend upon personal choice. Personal choices can change only when people change internally, and this requires moral and spiritual development. What will change a racist? The modern world has no solution to this problem and can only hope to contain it. Even the prevention strategy of anti-racist education cannot guarantee that the next generation will be less racist, or that 'racialism' will not crop up in another form, at another conflict barrier in society, such as age, sex or nationality. Xenophobia can be finally rooted out only when xenophobes undergo moral and spiritual change. Similarly, the negative attitudes to the rest of society of groups living in a marginalized situation can evolve only as a function of all people beginning to change their attitudes, values, objectives or demands. Most contemporary prescriptions for social reform, on the other hand, assume that changes of this kind will occur as social structures and conditions alter, that is, as unemployment reduces, educational opportunities increase, anti-discrimination policies start to take effect, and so forth.

Thus, the argument flows into the area of the second proposition, and we anticipate solutions that are top-down. We begin to search for leadership that will cut through the propaganda of social polarizations. Education is thus one of our main hopes, and we look for enlightened values and teaching in education to ensure that the schools come to the aid of society. Because so many other factors enter into people's education, we also look to new alliances between schools and parents, schools and employers, schools and social services, and to new curricula that tackle controversial issues courageously, and new pedagogical approaches that encourage more active participation by learners, in the belief that personally and collectively we will discover solutions that an administrative system has not discovered. Spontaneity and creativity complement rationality. Society solves its problems to a considerable extent by an ongoing process of brainstorming, a technique which suffers from a misnomer, since its processes actually place much reliance upon the affective, the heart as much as the mind. In education, therefore, everything comes to a focus upon teachers, who must be the real philosophers of education, the initiators of its reform, and consequently key contributors to social reform in general.

Greatly telescoped, this is the liberal democratic solution, not the radical one of either right or left which are both structural and thus deny the essence of what is being argued here. But the characteristic feature of the liberal democratic solution, combining as it does the rational and the holistic dimensions, is its insistence upon self-reliance, upon conscious human energy to bring about social change. Structuralists despise such notions, which they see as ignoring the enduring realities of economics and politically patterned behaviour, while the socially disadvantaged see the need for something more comprehensive, more reflective of grassroots demands. Because of the patent failure of their policies to prove themselves effective, disillusionment pervades the liberal democratic camp in contemporary society. It is at this point that many are prepared to acknowledge the spiritual dimension and acknowledge that we are in spiritual crisis, and that we need to look again at what religious groups and the churches are saying as one way of enlisting the generosity or idealism of people, especially the young, who can believe in the possibility of a better world.

But what happens if we turn this argument around and, instead of beginning from the rational and proceeding to the holistic and the spiritual, we begin from the spiritual? If, as has been argued, our spiritual nature is primary, then our first insight is into the basic contradictions of society in which so much energy goes towards setting up and maintaining the idols of wealth, power, status and scientific knowledge. The fundamental pathology of society is then seen to be neither structural nor philosophical, but moral. Each of the five propositions can be taken in quite another way if we turn them upon ourselves and ask what we may be doing that either validates or challenges them. In so far as we engage in material striving, group competition, or social repression, we validate the first three propositions; in so far as we feel ourselves morally or spiritually challenged to see these contradictions and to dissolve them, we validate the last two propositions. And this in turn leads to acknowledging alternatives for the worlds of education, public policy and social relationships that depend on a more widely diffused acceptance of personal responsibility.

What are the characteristics of this spiritual vision that can positively challenge alternative perspectives? Several points can be cited. First of all, there is the heartfelt truth, whether it comes as intuition, creative impulse or as an inspiration, which makes the spiritual decisive; decisive to the point of self-sacrifice, for example. In this, the spiritual transcends the balancing acts of liberal democracy. It can be radically decisive. Further, the spiritual can respect the value of the rational and the holistic. Although primary, it can acknowledge the fact of the incarnate, that is, of the legitimacy of the demands of mind, heart and body, and of the organic unity of all of these. And, thirdly, the spiritual represents not simply human interests but the presence of God in creation, and therefore the spiritual cannot authentically be enlisted to serve human rivalries. This means that the spiritual cannot be divided against itself and must always see a higher order unity, even where there is lower order division, including of course moral evil. The spiritual, when confronted by competing views, demands and offers respect and dialogue.

It is only through the spiritual that we can find radical reconciliation, whether within ourselves or with others. It is worth pondering that all the main religions agree that spiritual peace must begin in individuals' hearts and then diffuse outwards. Why should such a powerful insight be ignored by human intelligence and emotions? Undoubtedly this is the question that leads us to the heart of the spiritual perception of good and evil. We are spiritually disempowered, and it is to spiritual re-empowerment that education most needs to generate commitment.

Opening to the absolute

The rational world-view in education has to do with distinction and fragmentation, dividing to understand. The holistic world-view has to do with integrating, systemically relating, in order to comprehend. The spiritual world has to do with completing, in order to arrive at truth, perfection, or holiness. The Christian vision of the Incarnation has exactly this character. The divine gift is the gift of peace. Those who report spiritual experiences, and experiences of the transcendent, most often speak of the sense of peace they encounter (Hay, 1987: 150). Our rediscovery of the spiritual will not be the result of a change in fashion or of some sociological or political transformation. It will come directly to each individual, and from individual to individual, as a blessing. As we recognize our own inner self, so we recognize another's. When we learn to respect the uniqueness of the other we paradoxically recognize our common purpose, which is of the spiritual and not the material order. So many of the accounts people give of the spiritual emphasize the universal harmony, the sense of oneness that they feel. And of course peace is oneness; that is its most fundamental quality.

In our search for a way of speaking about the authentic spiritual understanding of education, or of any other aspect of human life, we cannot be satisfied with anything less than a reconciliation of the rational, the holistic and the spiritual. It may therefore be that, rather than as overlapping circles, we can better represent the Map of the Values Terrain as a set of concentric circles, the rational inside the holistic, which is in turn inside the spiritual. The spiritual is the context, the primary reality, the absolute. The nerve centre of society is not the Government, the school system, or even the Church, but the conscious human spirit experiencing unity of heart and mind, both in itself and with each and every other spirit, including the divine. Polarization is meaningless. Conflict may sometimes reveal partial truths but in fact it leads in the end to further conflict. The Marxist dialectic is only a case in point. By recovering a spiritual vision of the oneness of reality in its secular and spiritual dimensions, education can find the vital and creative power which comes only from a sense of meaning and purpose.

These contentions can neither be proved nor disproved. As matters of belief, they can only be chosen or refused. But it is on this basis that the final chapter of this book sets out to question current educational practice and to explore practical alternatives. It is for those who hold to the view that there is no such thing as a taboo on the spiritual, but only a victory of rational thinking over self-delusion, to decide whether they have any 'reason' to pursue such an enquiry. Undoubtedly, however, those who have had some intimation of the transcendent, the numinous, or the spiritual, and who are searching for a way to transfer this experience into the flesh and blood world of education, can both share this exploration and enhance it by their participation.

I have become aware from my experience of in-service training for teachers that many can no longer abide the vacant stare of rational–scientific education, or the voiceless echo of cosmic holism. They sense very clearly that love is the spiritual reality that provides essential unity of purpose and reconciles the apparently divided. They suffer from the fact that education itself has forsaken its essential vocation of seeking truth and wisdom (which have nothing to do with intellectualism), and enhancing the human person. According to the prevailing materialistic and utilitarian vision, *having* is more important than *being*, and educators are puppets of the economy or the state with no encouragement to believe in their vocation to reflect, criticize, enquire, warn, urge, or to commit themselves to something that is timeless rather than timely. Where this 'something' is perceived, however, it can be directly linked to central insights of the major world faiths, and nowhere more powerfully than to the Christian understanding of God in Jesus, the 'sign which shall be spoken against'.

It is because of the deep unease that can be found in so many teachers, who sense that education is at a watershed and must either go towards social functionality or towards what we must simply call spiritual enlightenment, that the recovery of the spiritual dimension of education has been taken as the central concern of this book. The argument is that we are coming back to an authentically spiritual view of reality, one in which there is a choice to be made between a power for ultimate good, on the one hand, and, on the other, private interests, material results, pride of position or intellectual arrogance. The choice to be made both opens up a new perspective of meaning, purpose and direction for education, and, I believe, can provide the radical energy needed for it really to make a difference in society.

Hope for the future

We cannot, however, leave the subject with no attempt being made to explore what the implications of such purposes might be for the practice of education. Indeed, it is impossible to evaluate the whole argument of this book if we do not make some attempt at this task. In any case, the importance of the spiritual vision derives not from our need to understand what has happened to our civilization, or even what is happening to us now, but from our responsibility to look towards the future. The future is essentially a matter of hope, since there is no way of knowing whether we even have a future beyond the instant at which I, the writer, am writing, or you, the reader, are reading. Hope is thus pre-eminently a spiritual quality. This can be discerned from considering the enormous weight of belief and trust being expressed by people in their plans and provisions for the future. All the deferred enjoyment in the present to gain more from the future, and all the reassurances we offer each other that things will change, that they will get better, must reflect the hope that we have, a kind of nostalgia for a state of being we have not yet known, but which is profoundly rooted in us.

It is our nature to seek *hopefully* to bring about a not yet existing state of affairs. The underlying impetus of this we call intention. It seems self-evidently good that we do prepare the future, for this is an expression of humanity's energies and creativity, but we can become so engrossed in our own efforts that we fail to recognize the realities which simultaneously constrain us. It is a problem for us to both intend and, at the same time, remain available to whatever else comes along. There is therefore a necessarily provisional quality about our attitudes and plans regarding the future. The future is a mystery. It haunts and enchants us. It beckons us and disdains us. It threatens and cajoles us. We have constantly to decide whether we are creating or fantasizing, whether we are seizing opportunities or being obsessional. The chance factor sometimes seems so large that nothing significant can be determined about the next stage of our lives, such as when there is an illness or an accident; yet at other times we see longed-for events turn out as we hoped. We think incessantly about the future, often looking only a matter of a few months ahead, sometimes a few years or more. But there is the looming question of where we are going at the end of it all. Is there a life beyond? How is our fate to be determined? We cannot resolve these conundrums, and we may reasonably choose not even to think about them, for the future is only available to us in hope.

We have been considering the faculties of mind, heart and spirit in this chapter, but of course these all find their human identity in a body. This is a central truth, one that is both scientific and religious. Scientifically, we cannot separate the elements of the person without losing part of the total reality. In religious terms, and especially in the incarnational perspective of Christianity, there is every justification for transcending disembodied theory, and regarding it as of ultimate value to work out our theory in a personal and physical context. This, in the practical educational sense, is the focus of the final chapter.

Chapter seven

The task: regenerating education

If the crisis of meaning in western society stems, as has been argued, from an absence of shared values other than those of secular materialism, then the taboo on discussion of the spiritual dimension of life is its most chronic symptom, and it is one that is readily apparent in education. Regardless of the intellectual difficulties, therefore, the main objective of this book has been to break the spiritual taboo in educational discussion, and the aim of this final chapter is to consider the relevance of the spiritual for educational policy and practice, in other words for the task of educational regeneration. The gravest concern is for those schools that ignore the spiritual, and flee from any positive statement of moral, ethical, spiritual or religious values, and in which achievement is seen in academic and vocational terms, or even as monetary guarantees, rather than as human or spiritual development.

Apart from its material goals, education is increasingly rootless, anomic and directionless because, it is contended, the larger existential questions are being avoided and false assumptions about the world fostered. Absolute values relating to the religious quest, truth and goodness are simply treated as meaningless, yet for any of these a person might one day have to decide whether or not to give their life. Indeed, there is a radical choice to be made between the secular and the spiritual, for there is no bridging continuum of attitudes. The spiritual is a leap apparently in the dark, a leap for which, as has been repeatedly said here, there is no adequate rational justification. On the other hand, education in the western world seems on the verge of an even more frightening void, because it is forgetting the crucible of faith and service from which the work of education emerged in the middle ages, and is becoming intoxicated with secular materialist values which, from a perspective of religious spirituality, equate to a form of idolatry.

Many teachers might accept that there is at least a moral argument for going against this materialist trend. First, it could be argued, young people have a right to engage with spiritual insights and to encounter what some believe to be the highest sources of meaning and purpose in life. Second, young people undoubtedly have a need to work out their own values and view-points, and to choose their own lifestyles, but to do this they need to see the alternatives. And, third, there is enough evidence that young people have a real desire to involve themselves in a spiritual search as a journey of discovery carried out in freedom. In view of this, educators have a responsibility not to abandon the young, as has happened so much in the last couple of generations, and instead to bring them the support and stimulus of a worked-out educational programme in both secular and spiritual dimensions.

The practical relevance of the spiritual to education, whether in formal or informal senses, lies in its challenge not only to qualitative aspects of the work of schools, such as the values that underlie their policy-making processes and working relationships, but also to the way the curriculum is built, and to how teachers are prepared, or prepare themselves for their work. This is not to say that the task of transforming education in line with the spiritually-centred vision proposed in the last chapter can be conceived only in this format, but that it will be here simply to have a means of dealing with educational and spiritual realities that allows communication through the printed word. It is certain that there are far better ways of sharing insights when people are actually in one another's presence.

The claims of a spiritual perspective

For teachers to seek to identify their own educational values and purposes thoroughly is a surprisingly rare occurrence. A notable example was in the Curriculum Enquiry 11–16 project, in which one of the procedures followed by the forty schools involved was to work out their aims, at school and departmental levels. This showed up some striking discrepancies, even cases where the headteacher claimed as aims of the school, views of his own that he had not previously communicated to the staff (Morgan, 1988). It is a more fundamental task to investigate personal values, and the author's experience of doing this with numerous groups of teachers over a period of twenty years of in-service teacher education has indicated that these matters have usually not been seriously considered either in initial training or in everyday professional life. Teachers have tended to see their work in terms of the content and level of specialist input rather than as the consequence of personally-held values which they have put into practice.

Some might argue that there is little point to such exercises when teachers are hired for specified responsibilities and not so that they should invent their own, but the fact is that problems arise in areas where value choices have got to be made, and where not to make a choice is to make a choice for prevailing values. Such a response cannot be equated with the traditional understanding of what is expected of, or for that matter by, professional workers. Those who have not reflected to see the kinds of people they are, and the kinds of influences they have become subject to, risk remaining mesmerized by other people's values and beliefs. They are thus either shamed into conformity or lulled into a flattering self-image, such as that they are modern, liberal, productive teachers, when they may well be culturally conditioned, ideologically repressive and spiritually blind. Either individually or with their colleagues, teachers need to examine the values that they are living and working by, to find out what these are, and to decide whether they are appropriate or need to be modified.

Teachers working in the same institution can have different personal values and different educational purposes, often without being aware of it. While there is no argument to be made for unthinking conformity of values, there is every justification for raising awareness about value discrepancies, so that at least the right hand knows what the left hand is doing. Ideally, a school in the Curriculum Enquiry project worked towards defining a core of shared values, a standpoint upon which all staff could agree. The project in fact reported a set of aims which were endorsed by high proportions of teachers in the schools surveyed (DES, 1983: 28). As a minimum, it would seem that teachers need opportunities and procedures to engage in reflection, to exchange views, possibly to influence each other, but in any case to take into account in their educational planning the various purposes at work among them.

The question is whether there are ways to encourage people to change their values and ways of teaching when they start from a position of being unmotivated or unwilling to do so. The key to this must surely lie in the collective approach of whole school thinking and planning. Courses of study can only stimulate and support school-based processes, even if individuals can sometimes undergo major experiences of personal development during extended post-experience training. Teachers who have not had such opportunities cannot be forced to change, and forced change would be valueless in any case. People can be convinced by argument, but still not change, often because of their feelings of threat or fear. But the hope is that observing their colleagues working consistently and collaboratively in new ways will inspire trust and commitment to change. The challenge is thus to teachers both individually and collectively. And the challenge is at the level of values and commitment even more than competence or knowledge. This is why the ideology of training, which is currently regaining ground in teacher education policy, is fundamentally misconceived. Teachers need strategies and fully understood modes of approach to the working out of their own educational values and aims.

How can the staff of a history department in a school teach their subject without paying any attention to the place of values in what they are doing? How will a particular pupil cope with teachers of widely differing values in relation to imperialism, developing societies, monarchy, nationalism or Marxism? As personal experience surely teaches us, it can be years before pupils wake up to the fact that their teachers have their own values and prejudices. It does no good to ignore problems of controversial issues in the curriculum. There is a moral responsibility to bring the matter of values out into the open amongst colleagues, and to allow their discussion. Teachers will then know where they stand, what support there is for particular perspectives, and community attitudes can be better taken into account in the teaching of controversial matters. The first step, though, is for the professionals to undertake their own reflection on values, and this can lead to wider institutional and community self-evaluation as a starting-point for more solid curriculum development.

Recent years have witnessed the development of many initiatives to support teachers in such work in Britain. These include a programme on the teaching of controversial issues in schools by the short-lived School Curriculum Development Committee, and several conferences of the Farmington Institute and the recently-formed National Association for Values in Education and Training. At the same time there have been research and development projects, such as the University of Hull Social Values Research Centre and the DES–Christian Education Movement 'RE Values' project on beliefs and values in secondary schools, which are feeding into staff development networks.

The purpose of more than twenty conferences for teachers that I have personally been involved in organizing on the theme of 'values in education' has been to encourage teachers to recognize and accept their cultural and spiritual responsibilities in developing schools and teaching based upon thought–through values. The thematic content has included the exploration of topics such as: the school and values; personal, social and moral education; teaching about Aids; peace in the school; education for one world; and holistic models of education and health. There has also been a series of conferences at Southampton University since 1984 with more specifically spiritual themes or approaches, including: spiritual values and education; beliefs and values; creativity and the spiritual; and, active learning in the spiritual area of experience. The teachers who have been most closely involved in these conferences have tended to agree that such issues, which they affirmed to be largely ignored by schools and by official teacher training, have direct relevance for the development of young people as morally and spiritually conscious beings. However, this was difficult, even dangerous territory for teachers, because the same questions were of concern to parents and to the wider community, and teachers felt subject to intense scrutiny when they took up such potentially contentious issues. In fact, teachers needed the support and legitimation of governors, local education authorities and parents if they were to do the work needed to meet genuine existential needs of the young.

A vitally important area of staff development is the training of school leaders, and especially of headteachers who have the main responsibility for developing the overall philosophy and organization of the school. The prime duty of the leader is to identify the goals of the institution, and the direction in which it is to go. This task involves the reconciliation of the many views that may coexist within the institution and its political environment, ensuring that every member of staff feels that they count, the successful linking of school and community, and the carrying into practice of the planned programme. Whether a school is run for the convenience of its staff or whether it serves an important purpose in the lives of its pupils will depend above all upon the moral and spiritual integrity of the headteacher.

It may appear that what is being said is that a value consensus can be built out of rational consultation and discussion, but this is problematic. The central value likely to emerge in this way is neutrality, a relativist position that agrees to respect differences, but which can only provide a basis for the lowest common denominator of educational priorities. By such means there is no hope of achieving a society that is collectively on other than moral shifting sands, however clear individuals are about their personal positions or interests. The radical alternative is to re-examine what was once taken for granted and can still be believed in absolutely, namely, the proposition that there is a source of ultimate values. The necessary corollaries are that we can know such values only by non-rational means, that is by intuition and faith, that we use such terms as ultimate values, truth, and absolute only in relation to a transcendent reality, which is spiritual in nature, and for many is to be called God; and, finally, that this argument is not reducible to social or psychological propositions or evidence. This alternative approach to identifying some of the central values and purposes of education, although it cannot be rationalized, can be validated out of the deepest levels of personal experience and conviction.

Everything that we find people calling the inner self, conscience, truth, trust, inner peace, holiness, 'beckoning goodness', as well as God, a power, a presence, the numinous, answers to prayer, faith and belief, are everyday reminders of what seems to have been forgotten or repressed, and yet remains part of our nature, part of what we are unavoidably concerned with in educating. Taken alone, such matters may seem too 'other-worldly' to be relevant to state education systems, but if they are totally excluded from our curriculum considerations, I cannot see a way forward from current polarizations. The spiritual perspective, I would contend as a basis for discussion, can contribute at least the following vital principles to education:

the ultimate responsibility that individuals have for themselves and for their action in society;

the need to restore the person to the centre of educational concerns, rather than the state, the economy, or any materialist ideology;

the centrality of the values of human life and fraternity in how we decide our personal actions or appraise the actions of others;

the equality of men and women everywhere, regardless of historical or racial distinctions, and their consequent rights to survival, to opportunities for self-determination, and to the development of their individual and social potentials;

that life is a process with a real destination, whether we see that destination in moral terms alone or as an after-life;

the value of humanity's perennial struggle towards peace, inter-group understanding, health, knowledge, and the provision of food and resources to meet needs;

the importance of every individual's will and contribution, and therefore of the opportunities offered to all to develop not just a personal, but a global moral vision;

the primacy of the spiritual nature of the human being, both in the individual's inner world and as shared with other persons.

The claims of a spiritual perspective have been firmly acknowledged in the British Education Reform Act 1988. Not only must a spiritual principle underlie the whole curriculum, according to the Act (Clause 1(2)(a)), but strong provisions relating to religious education and acts of collective worship in schools were inserted as amendments to the Bill during its passage through the House of Lords. So significant are these provisions that opportunities for subject-based and cross-curricular work in moral, spiritual and religious areas are potentially very greatly expanded. This effectively means that teachers of all disciplines are presented with new openings for involvement in beliefs and values curricula, since RE teachers will be adequate neither in number nor competence to cope with the developments required by the Act (Plunkett, 1989).

Work of the kind that is now needed has long formed part of the curriculum of denominational schools; and while not all are effective in developing such a perspective some are impressively so. At St Peter's Roman Catholic School, Bournemouth, for example, a curriculum philosophy has been worked out collectively by the staff which makes clear their shared responsibility to contribute to the moral, spiritual and religious development, not only of the pupils, but of the whole school community. The experience of this particular school is worth attention, not necessarily because it provides a model, but because it has gone through a relatively thorough process of review and consultation before the school and curriculum aims were set down (see Annexe 1). Over a two-year period there was a series of meetings of a school curriculum committee and of staff groups – for example on multi-cultural education and on economic awareness – and of the whole staff meeting together with an external consultant. Since the school is Catholic, the overall spiritual perspective contained in its six fundamental principles and its school aims is much more explicit than that which might be adopted in most schools in the British system, and yet the example is effective in indicating how it is possible to work towards a practical outcome from a strong and uncompromising spiritual starting-point.

In some ways the task of accommodating the spiritual might be easier for schools where the specifically religious component was being less emphasized. An example of a school which has developed along similar lines to St Peter's in its processes of review and staff participation in drawing up a common philosophy is Horndean Comprehensive School, near Portsmouth, where the values are much more clearly mainstream (see Annexe 2). There, too, the process of refinement of the school philosophy is an ongoing one. Horndean, for example, finds itself facing many different priorities, and has staff working parties to review such areas as information technology, equal opportunities and learning support. As this work is completed, and as the curriculum is further developed, there will be new implications for the statement of the school's general aims. The emphasis given to moral, spiritual and religious concerns will depend only in outline upon the national legislative framework, and much more directly upon the commitment of teachers, individually and collectively.

However, a coherent curricular basis for learning requires more than mere discussion among the staff of a school, though this is the beginning of it. A high level of participation by teachers is not easy to achieve; there are always reluctant participants. It used to be said that the teacher in England enjoyed a high degree of autonomy. I do not think that this is being said any longer, but I wonder how true it has ever been. Teachers may have had freedom on a given day in a given classroom, but they neither decided their own timetable, chose their own pupils, controlled their own resources, nor were they able to remain indifferent to test or examination results. The autonomy teachers had, and basically still have, consists in a certain personal privacy. It may be that they will be obliged to forego this privacy if they want to increase their genuine professional standing. By working in groups and teams, teachers are in a stronger position to affect the curriculum. They do not need to develop totalitarian control, but to become a nerve centre of awareness about what is going on in the school and what needs to go on. In this way they can develop an operating framework within which a degree of elasticity is retained.

By working in this way, teachers are not merely following a rational model but are expressing their own values and intentions. Moreover, they are giving effect to the notion of the school as an organic body; they are moving towards a holistic view of the school. Phrases abound to describe such schools as 'thinking schools', 'self-evaluating schools', and so forth, but an overly rational and teacher-centred view of schooling is misleading. From the earliest studies in educational sociology it has consistently been shown that a conflict model of the school, representing the opposition of teacher and pupil interests, allows for a more complete analysis than a consensus model (Waller, 1932). Even if pupils do not inevitably oppose teachers, it is found to be the case in all the classic researches in this field that oppositional groups arise within schools and produce what is effectively a subculture polarized with respect to teachers' official views (Hargreaves, 1967; Lacey, 1970; Willis, 1977). Apart from pupils' alternatives to official values, there are unspoken, and even unthought out teacher values that are reflected in rules, attitudes shown in informal situations, and customs, many of them not stemming from teachers, which together form a hidden curriculum which can provide as powerful a learning experience as that which is made explicit, or is required by the institution.

Instead of lamenting that the schools seem unable to realize their full potential, it is worth asking whether teachers are sufficiently forthright in making known their values and beliefs. If teachers espouse neutrality out of fear of offending colleagues, pupils, parents, and others who may have different values and commitments, they are denying their own right to equal respect. In any case, so often such fears are the result of untested assumptions about where others stand. It is far safer for humanity in the long term, for teachers to acknowledge their own values and beliefs rather than to risk surrendering to official values, such as those of the enterprise culture, or, as is otherwise bound to happen, indoctrinating in unacknowledged values or indeed in relativism. The best chance for spiritual values to play their part in educational decisions would lie in teachers being committed to a genuine openness and to the critical affirmation of the views that emerged.

Building the spiritual into the whole curriculum

The curriculum may be thought of as the school's output, in the sense that this is the justification publicly accepted for schools. But even the term curriculum is ambiguous. For some, it is the sum total of the teaching subjects timetabled, whereas others would argue for a holistic notion, where the whole is greater than the sum of the parts. According to this view, in studying a curriculum, a pupil does not merely add up a set of fragmented subjects, but samples from a map of knowledge or a culture. Thus, for example, a pupil will often learn thinking skills, aesthetic standards, religious values, health care, interpersonal qualities, and so forth, not from a specific subject but from the pervasive effects of multiple, and often uncoordinated inputs into the total programme. Progressive professional thinking has in recent years sought to make the notion of the 'whole curriculum' more prominent (DES, 1969; DES, 1983). In the Curriculum Enquiry 11–16 project, it was seen as the role of the whole school staff to plan the curriculum within a framework of understanding of the place of different subjects, skills, values, concepts and information. Such a notion reconciled rationalist and holistic approaches. This idea prospered in official policy in British education of the 1970s in the shape of the 'core' curriculum. Although there were different versions of the core, they had in common the idea that a set of important areas of learning should be guaranteed, not left to chance according to individuals' selections of subjects of study.

In its most radical form the core curriculum abandoned specific subjects altogether. Some programmes of study for the transition phase from compulsory schooling to adult and working life, such as TVEI, the Certificate of Pre-vocational Education and the Youth Training Scheme, had a number of general aims which were to be ensured not through separate teaching but by integrated learning, for example through projects and experience-based learning exercises. The merit claimed for such innovations was that they allowed both for conventional learning of desired content, as with subjects, and for curriculum-wide skills and attitudes that were important for everyday life. Instead of the traditional subject curriculum, with its vertically segregated elements, the core allowed for vertical and horizontal elements which could be adjusted to the needs of learners. One current theme of academic debate in education is essentially about the validity of such core models, as compared with those that specify subject content much more precisely and leave much of the horizontal element, for example in personal, health, careers, social, moral and spiritual development, to the professional conscience of teachers.

It is difficult to comprehend how the breadth and balance claimed for the national curriculum prescribed by the 1988 Education Reform Act in England and Wales will rival what has been achieved by the best practice according to alternative models. Knowledge and understanding can be readily specified by subject labels, and can be tested, but it is doubtful if a testing system can ever attach significant status to skill learning, even less to attitudinal elements in the curriculum, and least of all to those skills and attitudes that are expected to be acquired by voluntary and unresourced cross-curricular osmosis. The areas of learning that are most in danger are precisely those that the spiritual perspective would bring into focus, that is, personal values, aesthetic and creative qualities, sensitive issues in daily living, problems in maturation and personal development, basic philosophical concerns about meanings and priorities in life, and so forth. Many of these matters are referred to in the special issue of the *British Journal of Religious Education*, of 1985, on the theme of 'Spirituality across the curriculum', but it is not apparent that they are seriously addressed by official policies on the curriculum. In fact, the gap between the pragmatic and the spiritual understanding of life is here seen at its widest in the educational field: most official documents and academic texts that comprise the curriculum literature severely neglect the spiritual dimension if they do not ignore it entirely.

The curriculum has become an instrument of economic and social policy when it should be just as much a spiritual celebration of humanity's inner and outer beauty. We are now at a point of philistinism at which the curriculum is seen as an investment to harvest material benefits for society rather than as a way of empowering people in their own odysseys of reflection and life. Non-materialist aims of education echo emptily in public documents and politicians' speeches, but where they have no substance or intention behind them, they bind no one, either morally or politically. When the staff of St Peter's School discussed their curriculum response to pressures for economic awareness teaching, however, they faced a serious issue about the degree to which such developments could be harmonized with the spiritually-based philosophy the school had adopted.

In the case of both its spiritual and aesthetic dimensions, the contemporary school curriculum has lost definition, and has tended to become a rag-bag of cultural relics. For example, it might be thought to be obvious how essential the spiritual dimension is to the creative aspect of the curriculum. As we approach the creative in anything other than materialist terms we are coming up against an unknown. The unknown may simply be our own hidden talents in painting, writing, performing, or just simply thinking, or it may be some greater force so far defying rational or any other explanation. In spiritual terms anyone trusting their own creativity must face uncertainty, make themselves open to a mystery, and allow themselves to be vulnerable. Thus, the creative is guided by values that involve a risking of identity and of personal security, but also a prospect of insight, self-knowledge, sensitivity, and a more profound experience of what it is to be human and what it means to receive grace. In other words, the creative can be a direct channel into the spiritual.

How might a curriculum evolve a concern with spiritual values? There are many countries in which deliberate values education has played a prominent part in the curriculum, for example Sweden among the western nations and Tanzania among third world societies. However, beyond such planned curriculum projects, schools inevitably act as carriers of values of a political, economic, social, moral or other kind, and usually have a function of indoctrinating in favour of a dominant social view. The extent to which curricula can be pointed in other directions to bring about value change desired by minorities is unclear. Direct values teaching can be counter-productive. Altering content may not have a strong effect, but changes in teaching methods may be more influential. That is to say that the curriculum of itself may not be an effective means of value change unless is it part of a whole educational programme. A significant illustration arises in connection with current anxieties about Aids education, and perhaps this provides an opportunity to suggest in the most practical terms what part the spiritual might play in relevant curriculum development.

The immediate reaction to the Aids scare in Britain was a barrage of TV announcements and teaching materials which were nothing less than propaganda for 'safe sex' – a far from neutral notion. This was followed by the development of materials providing information, that went beyond the pamphleteering phase and sought to deal with queries of a factual, non-specialist nature. A third stage was reached when schools liaised with external agencies to provide group and individual guidance and counselling, to help young people to see the threat of Aids in a serious light, and to refer them where necessary to more specialized bodies. A fourth stage involved the more systematic exploration of the subject through ethically neutral analysis of the reality of Aids in the community, how it is spread, and what patterns of social and sexual life are associated with risk of infection. These four stages of the development of public understanding and education have been seen by many educators and politicians as the way by which the spread of the disease can be controlled. There is however a fifth stage about which most commentators have tended to be extremely squeamish, and that is to deal with Aids as a moral and spiritual issue. Catching Aids, or not catching it, whether secret testing is ethical, whether partners should be told about an infection, living with it or with people who have it, or dying from it, are all matters of moral and spiritual concern in their own right, as well as being pointers to broader moral and spiritual issues of which Aids is only an example.

Another critical values issue is the teacher's response to the multi-faith society. There are those who speak of post-Christian society, as if this meant that Christian values had been replaced by some alternative and that it is no longer possible to look to Christianity for spiritual insights to indicate meaning, direction and purpose in life. This would be the equivalent of throwing away two thousand years of history. There is however no reason why the co-existence of other faiths should diminish the expression of Christian beliefs, values and virtues. On the contrary, religions can stimulate each other, and the zeal with which Muslims, Hindus, Buddhists and others live their faiths should only encourage Christians to clarify what they believe and live. New interfaces are forming in our societies. British Christians may understand Sikh attitudes to life better than those of lifelong friends who have abandoned Christianity for secular materialism. Believing Christians easily find common traits with practising Jews. In the same way, with many adherents of different world faiths they will have a closer agreement on the part that spiritual insights should play in the curriculum than with those who declare themselves relativists or agnostics.

This contribution to values education from a number of different faiths is vital to contemporary western societies, because secular pluralism offers no clear signals to schools. More generally, professional concern about teaching controversial issues all too often eventuates in a values agnosticism, which abandons substance in favour of strategies of procedural neutrality, or the demonstration of fairness to all views (Stradling *et al.*, 1984). This is a game rather than a serious solution because it reinforces the very relativism that has occasioned the problem in the first place. The controversial implies a mish-mash of views, none of them actually important because nothing is to be decided. It may be more useful to speak of 'contentious' issues in which it is legitimate to recognize a diversity of truths, where each one matters to whoever holds it, including the teacher. If these issues fall into such categories as finding meaning and purpose in life, civil and human rights, ideologies of conflict and nationalism, inequalities, pluralism and sectarianism, sexual ethics and morals, or the field of culture, media and leisure, just to pick some obvious areas, then it rapidly becomes clear that the traditional curriculum is planned neither to deal comprehensively nor adequately with them. Is there any alternative to a critical ethical, moral and spiritual appraisal of issues that arise in these areas? Is there a spiritual perspective on such potential curriculum topics that takes us beyond the liberal–progressive consensus?

By any definition in common use the spiritual surely cannot be consigned to a part of the curriculum, such as religious education, and thus banished from other subject areas. Like the rational and the holistic, the spiritual is a dimension to human awareness and, as such, belongs to every aspect of knowledge and must permeate the curriculum. This contention does of course imply that the spiritual can be rendered very vulnerable to neglect. If it were to be thought of only in the context of religious education, then it has as good a chance as religious education of gaining attention. But if it is to be buried in the synthesis of elements that go to make up the whole curriculum, then it can be ignored, or down-played. Rational or holistic approaches to issues do not necessitate spiritual awareness. How then can its cross-curricular claims be justified? The point of the spiritual in the curriculum is that we should be reminded of and helped to recognize our essentially spiritual nature by all our learning, whether in the humanities, the sciences, the social sciences or the arts. The tendency to make rational and utilitarian considerations sufficient, and to foreclose discussion of spiritual insights, does not do away with the spiritual dimension, but merely masks it. The spiritual, though mysterious, remains part of our everyday life. We may not be ready to advert to this as a society, but those teachers who do feel ready must surely trust their insights and seek to bring them back into the public domain in their field of work.

The spiritually attuned teacher

As is often said, there is a sense in which teachers are the curriculum. Not only are their teaching and learning approaches of critical importance, but the quality of the personal relationship established between teacher and taught is a vital aspect of the latter's learning. This was well recognized in traditional independent education in Britain, but translating this into large comprehensive schools with changes of teacher every hour or so is a serious educational undertaking. How are teachers burdened with test deadlines going to build the relationships that will be positive and empowering for young people lacking self-awareness and confidence, especially if we are thinking of the whole range of pupils and not just the elite?

What would it mean to teach with the utter conviction that the learner was body, mind, heart and spirit? This holistic view of the learner would encourage us to respect his or her individuality, to be student-centred, to be attentive to specific needs and talents, and to ensure that the content of teaching did not pre-empt the learner's preferences and initiatives. This implies not only 'the subordination of teaching to learning'

(Gattegno, 1970), but also a kind of teaching that inevitably opens up the private sphere rather than merely dealing with prepared material. Fundamentally, such pedagogies involve listening and the kind of dialogue among equals that Freire proposes (Freire, 1972). If teachers have their own projects too much at heart, they cannot be available to the learner. Listening involves more than just capturing the spoken word. Full listening involves being with the other with empathy, experiencing with them, sensing the other as a complete human being, with the depth of beliefs, hopes, fears and other senses and feelings that make up a whole personality, and then responding to the core of the person. In such circumstances we can experience the creativity and generative power of human relationships. Of course there are obvious implications for the size of teaching groups, but should this kind of experience be denied teachers and students in schools, especially at a time when so many young people experience feelings of alienation and rejection in society?

More particularly, seeing that teachers are given such authority over the young, and are continually being asked to assess, select, rank and judge them, is it not fruitful to question such procedures, and to suggest the value of the complete opposite? Teachers could acknowledge the potentials, the talents, the contributions of learners. They could question the habitual assessing and judging, the finding of faults and weaknesses, the treating of learners as objects, even problems. It is an illusion for teachers to behave as if they were invulnerable, independent leaders, as if they were not dependent for everything they do on the resources, inspiration, skills or commitment of others. All that we do, for good or ill, is rooted in our human identity and community, with others as our strength and deserving of our appreciation and care. What teachers can honestly say that they receive nothing from their students. Or, if they should claim that they do not, then how are they teaching, and what are their students getting out of it?

Why do more teachers not adopt student-centred views and approaches? Part of the reason must be because they have not fully understood what is involved. And this in turn must be because they have not achieved a high degree of self-awareness, including insight into their own learning and development processes, which could serve as the base for their own pedagogical knowledge. Good theories have their value, but teaching is learnt less as a theoretical science than as the result of personal experience and reflection. If it is only reaction to experience, the danger is that it will simply mirror what has previously occurred; likewise it cannot be simply the result of reflection. The beginning of effective teaching must lie in knowledge of the self, and yet this is a dimension that is virtually ignored in initial teacher education.

In-service courses in counselling, experiential learning, life skills teaching, pastoral care, and the like, may counter-balance this to some extent, but these are often courses for the already convinced. Many teachers have found that courses in Rogerian counselling, Berne's transactional analysis and scripts, values clarification, co-counselling, Gestalt therapy, or other forms of interpersonal and group development, have helped lead them to a re-thinking of their values and ways of relating to others.

There are many, including teachers, who are frightened by the prospect of self-knowledge, and yet without it we are inevitably slaves to whatever instincts, habits, prejudices and passions we have unwittingly inherited or developed. It is for this reason that indoctrination can never pass for education. If as a teacher I have only my own view of things, only my own way of proceeding, my own interpretation of events, and my own standards, with no give, no genuine concern to accommodate my students, to discover their contribution, to learn from them, what can I expect? Either I shall completely overrun them, have my own way and cripple their confidence and self-esteem, or I shall find myself locked in conflict with them. If, on the other hand, I approach teaching with a position worked out in broad outline, clear about my principles and priorities, well briefed with my arguments and data, but ready to listen and to dialogue, aware that the whole truth necessarily escapes me, and believing in the right of others to have their view and to be satisfied that they are respected, then the teaching situation becomes both more dynamic and more fruitful.

Note that this argument does not excuse the teacher from being competent and authoritative, for that is the responsibility of any teacher. The point is that the teacher's knowledge can never be sufficient to erase the individuality of the learner. There has been considerable disquiet about the implied value of a negotiated approach in teaching. Negotiation as a curricular strategy cannot mean that the learner has an equal right to judge what the curriculum content and teaching approach should be. The matter cannot be posed in legalistic terms. It is a question rather of an ethical principle to be applied by the conscientious teacher to avoid all taint of indoctrination of the learner.

Our best teacher, as everyone can attest, is our own experience. Experience-based learning is immediate and personal. It involves activity and feelings. It allows learners responsibility for their own learning. And it leaves the initiative with the learner. Learning develops from experience both directly, for example through trial and error, and as a consequence of analysing and reflecting upon the experience that we have had. Such methods of learning can most productively be developed where teachers are aware of their potential and are able to introduce them spontaneously into their work. Teaching of this kind is in fact much more like everyday human relationships than the sometimes inflated language of educational studies might imply. There is hardly an area of learning in which some experiential element cannot be introduced or reinforced to extend the understanding or significance of concepts or ideas, and even more of attitudes and skills. Furthermore, experiential learning has an active quality, through which the learner can become aware, and discover and create their own learning. For this reason at least, from the teacher's point of view every learner is worthy of respect, attention and care.

Among the most striking examples of such an approach to teaching must be that of Jesus. The pedagogy reflected in the gospels is a surprisingly neglected theme, judged even from a secular viewpoint, and I do not have space here for more than a few key points that have struck me as a basis for further reflection. Jesus taught by example, by who he was and how he lived even more than by what he said. He respected the physical needs, state of mind and capabilities of those he was addressing. He frequently offered his teaching by indirect allusions and questioning, and did not attempt to impose it when it was questioned. He used the everyday experience of the disciple, either by direct reference or through the parable stories that reflected contemporary life. He did not urge propositions and conclusions so much as suggest illustrations and observations which people were then obliged to ponder. He challenged the disciple's imagination and intelligence with apt comment or scriptural quotation, with paradox, and with his clarity of vision.

It was also characteristic of his teaching that he drew attention constantly to the primacy of spiritual and moral over scientific truth, and that he dealt with the whole person with love and total immediacy. However unattainable such a standard may seem, it does provide powerful guidelines for any teacher, regardless of subject or beliefs. If we look at the example of pedagogy in the spiritual domain that Jesus gave, then it is even more clear how radically different his approach was from general contemporary practice. He was totally involved in a life of prayer, of self-giving, and of consciousness of the mission he had been given, and he constantly identified the spiritual significance of everyday reality.

Some teachers are now using exercises of meditation, or stilling, and encouraging attitudes of wonder and contemplation where possible in schools, as an alternative to the covering of content and the reaching of rational conclusions (Jones, 1986). The ideas that come in the quietness are often ones that were not being sought. Thinking too concentratedly can block this creativity. So much happens in moments of silence that it is not surprising if it entails a special openness to the spiritual. Though the emptiness of silence may disturb, there can be a sense of presence at such moments – not of course like a tactile presence, but akin to the known presence of another in the gaps in a telephone conversation. From the void of silence, even it seems in a school classroom, can also come the growing conviction of some transcendent presence or of some illumination (Beesley, 1988). The repeated practice of listening in stillness is not merely a technique for having good ideas, therefore, but it is the time-honoured way of becoming attuned to the spiritual dimension of life. It needs to be asked how far does education reflect the notion that the present moment is the most important, the moment that needs to be savoured, as opposed to the time that has to be sacrificed to some generalized future benefit? Such ideas are resisted, indeed often rejected, in contemporary society, so they demand courage and commitment from those who attach value to them and want to find opportunities of putting them into practice.

Education will not open up space to the spiritual unless teachers wish for this development. Teachers are the key mediators between the society and the rising generation. They have a unique role, and control significant cultural resources. If they defer to dominant economic and political values they will play no part in influencing what educational and social systems are aiming to achieve. But the counterpart of this is that they are in a position, if they so decide, to exercise an active moral and spiritual responsibility. Indeed, it seems that it is only if teachers decide for such a position that there is any prospect of transcending the polarized debates that currently paralyse education. How will teachers make up their minds? They need to return to a sense of their calling, to a spiritual sense of self, life and work. Although their job is in part defined for them by institutions and laws, they also discover their vocation out of the practical experience of teaching. It is in so far as the meaning and value of a person's existence transcends the role given to them by society that a spiritual dimension opens up in which an authentic vocation can be found. Otherwise there would be no issue to be resolved, and teachers would simply need to do their jobs faithfully according to the needs and prescriptions of society as determined by the public authorities.

As teachers discover their own vocations in this particular sense of the word they are able to recognize the spiritual callings of their students, and thus can become models for them. The overwhelming need is for teachers to be engaged in their own search, conscious of their own inner selves and aiming at realizing a greater integrity in their professional lives. Only personal values are real. Official values advertised by educational institutions are meaningless unless backed by the commitment of individual teachers. It is in so far as teachers are convinced and convincing in their personal values, behaviour and relationships that they can generate hope in those they teach. Therefore, whether the spiritual dimension is contained within us, or whether it transcends us, an awareness of the genuine in ourselves and others opens our hearts and minds to spiritual insight, and gives us grounds for hope.

Epilogue

'Each person who takes the faint path through the wilderness also helps somebody else to find the path.'

(A companion on a Dartmoor trail)

This book has been an exploration which is in many ways a personal one, linked to specific experiences and traditions; but it has seemed to me more valuable to write from within a lived set of beliefs and values, without wanting to declare them dogmatically, than simply to open up issues that are never thought of as being on the way to any resolution. Holding the view that life ultimately demands commitment to spiritual beliefs and values, I see this as being the most fundamental need of our societies, which have lost a sense of purpose and are moving into deeper crisis without any common basis for hope in the future. It is also my conviction that there is a change coming about, that a revival of spiritual values is occurring, even though it is not noticed by those who are not participating in it.

The basic spiritual insights about which there is wide agreement are positive, creative and hopeful notions about the meaningfulness of certain ultimate truths that give us an in-built check on the utilitarian and scientific values of the material order. Education seriously needs the stimulus of all who feel open to the spiritual dimension of existence if its practitioners and policy-makers are to take a long-term view of their purposes. Teachers who accept this spiritual movement have, I believe, a new opportunity to work, not as militants or propagandists, but as seekers and defenders of the human right of younger members of the society to form a personal view about the spiritual dimension to life, based upon reason, intuition, reflection and exchange.

It has been contended throughout this book that the importance of the spiritual is that it offers a unifying purpose, whether to education or to the whole of life. Historically, it is of course undeniable that factions and even nations have fought for spiritual causes, and the passions aroused by religious wars are probably unequalled. Does it follow that the spiritual is at the heart of such conflicts, or is it not that the radical power of the spiritual has been harnessed to national, racial and ideological strife? Spiritual power lies in the awareness of the oneness of reality not of its divisions. In Christian theology, this oneness is represented by Christ, who combines the timeless and the timely by being both God and man. The spiritual thus sounds the note of metaphysical hope that human divisions can be overcome because of the unity of the non-material context within which our present reality is believed to exist.   ·

Those who judge, blame or attack, are emphasizing divisions, indeed they are creating them. We can express ourselves negatively to the extent that that is literally all we do. And it may be that we live in a time when negative forces are being powerfully unleashed in society. Blame attaches to criminals, youth, governments, the police, the media, gays, financiers, workers, management, teachers, and so forth. The question is whether, with so many under attack, spiritual or religious beliefs are merely an opiate to help us disassociate ourselves from what we do not like, or whether they are part of a solution. The way to answer this question is to see what happens if we take the view opposite to the blaming one. If we look to see the positive qualities around us, in people and in how they help us by their attitudes, words and actions, what then happens? If someone says or does something that fills us with consolation or hope, or gives praise that is sincere, or delivers promised help, or brings moral strength when we feel weak, what interpretation are we to put on it? Is this just a service that we will be expected to repay? Or do we see in it a human quality of natural concern? Or as the reflection of divine qualities of love and mercy?

What happens at such moments? Do we not see some sign of transcendent goodness? Are these not the times when we feel that it is possible to believe in a spiritual power, and do we not respond to this by becoming more the kinds of people who take the initiative in seeing the positive in, and caring for others? From this too may come a growth in commitment to living by values that we do not wish to question. But this is not because we are conditioned, or because we feel constrained by external forces, or even by other people's expectations. The crucial element to commitment is the other *person* involved. It is to the other person, who could for religious believers be the divinity, that one is committed. It is to the other person that the idea of being faithful to the commitment is directed. Without this personal element, commitment risks being obsessional. And thus education, which now has all the riches of science at its disposal, all the potentialities of psychology, all the solicitations of industry, needs constantly to guard against being seduced away from its main commitment which is to people.

In keeping faith with our commitments we are undoubtedly helped by the human community around us. Other people who face the same challenges provide example, advice, support and insight which are of vital importance to us. This is because a genuine human community is formed by mutual loyalty in which family, friendship, work associates and other contacts have played their part. Similarly, teachers who decide that they will not blindly follow social, economic and political trends, but will form their own intentions, are helping to expand the moral and spiritual horizons of society. For some, it is enough to have rejected pragmatic and rationalist constraints, and their enlightenment comes from human sources only. But others believe that the spiritual contribution goes further, that it is the spiritual vision, the idea of a constant objective despite changing circumstances, that most truly inspires us, because it leads us, however uncertainly, along the faint path traced already by others, as well perhaps as by the One who, as the Psalmist puts it 'owns the earth and the fulness thereof'.

Some who do not discern this path may feel threatened by those who claim to do so, perhaps because they reject what they see as an attempt to reinstate unwelcome controls and reactionary forms of thought. The spiritual quest, reinforced by the rational and intuitive qualities that are so powerfully present in the contemporary world, is unlikely to mean a going back to any social or political system that has existed, but much more a carrying forward, into what is otherwise a very uncertain future, of the basic and perennial human qualities of hope and commitment which have lain behind every cycle of change and development, and which have always challenged the inertness of a particular age. The paradox of *our* time is that we have never believed so much that we were alive, when what we mainly are is busy, and never doubted so many fundamental truths, when we are so greatly in need of them for the survival and ultimate destiny of humanity.

Annexe 1

St Peter's School
School review and policy
(Extract from a school document)

The school's six fundamental principles are:

Its Christian foundation.
The formation of the whole person.
Recognition of the individual.
The school as a Christian community.
The central role of the teaching staff.
Partnership with the parents.

The aims of the school are expressed in terms of those experiences, achievements and accomplishments which we wish our pupils to take with them when they leave school. We wish our pupils to leave as mature and well-balanced young people, able to serve and to lead, and prepared to contribute positively to society in fulfilment of their own special calling. Thus we want them:

- To have experienced and at least begun to understand their dignity as persons.
- To have grown in faith and in the commitment to follow Christ and to communicate him to the world, through our teaching and example, the experience of prayer and liturgy, and the support of a Christian community.
- To have acquired a scale of values, as well as moral and social attitudes, in conformity with Christian teaching.
- To have developed qualities characteristic of the Christian, such as integrity, commitment, unselfishness, forbearance, compassion, joy.
- To have experienced the freedom that allows them to develop

initiative and creativity, and to grow in trustworthiness, personal responsibility and self-reliance.

- To have experienced the encouragement and success essential to building motivation, self-confidence and self-esteem.
- To have acquired the understanding, knowledge and skills relevant to adult life and employment.
- To have discovered and developed, to the best of their ability, their special gifts and talents, so that they can live full, happy and worthwhile lives.
- To have pursued excellence and achieved the highest standards of which they are capable by always giving of their best.
- To have developed lively, creative and enquiring minds and the desire to continue learning when they leave school.
- To have developed their critical faculties and judgement, and thus the ability to think for themselves, to make their own decisions and to manage their own lives.
- To have developed a sense of justice, a determination to overcome prejudice and a genuine concern for peace and understanding between races, religions and cultures
- To have developed a respect and concern for the integrity of others and the value of listening, understanding and generously offering service.
- To have learned to accept their responsibilities as both students and young people on the threshold of adulthood.
- To have discovered, in the light of faith, their own specific calling to live as responsible citizens and to participate constructively and productively in society.
- To have developed a profound politicial, social and civic awareness.
- To have accepted the challenge to be positive agents of change in a society that is continuously evolving.

Annexe 2

Horndean School
Aims of the school
(Extract from a school document)

As society changes in terms of its expectations, its standards of morality, its social and economic stresses and its priorities, so the school's curriculum must attempt to reflect this in that pupils need to be equipped to cope with the demands of the society into which they will emerge on leaving school.... However, there are a number of basic aims which remain constant:

- To create and sustain an ethos in the school in which there is a readily identifiable sense of stability and security in which pupils may find the sum total of their experience to be essentially enjoyable.
- To create an educational environment which will allow the ability, personality and character of each pupil to develop positively and appropriately.
- To stimulate in pupils a sustained sense of interest, curiosity and enquiry which will be reflected in the keenness and enthusiasm with which they undertake the work in hand.
- To enable each individual pupil to examine his/her position in relation to others and the views of others, and by the same token to seek and reach an understanding of the concept of cooperation, team-work and responsibility.
- To develop attitudes that will enhance the pupil's ability to work independently, in order to encourage self-discipline, self-confidence and a sense of responsibility.
- To encourage creativity, imagination and independence of mind in all aspects of the curriculum.
- To assist pupils in acquiring and developing skills which will

equip them to cope with a changing society, with problems and with new experiences.

- To prepare pupils to enter an adult world with all its varied values, pressures and obligations, particularly with regard to an appropriate approach to both employment and leisure time, whether the latter be enforced or in rest time.
- To give pupils learning opportunities in areas of knowledge and experience which will offer them relevant and useful information and with which they can form and express their own opinions.

References

Apple, M. (1986) *Teachers and Texts: a Political Economy of Class and Gender Relations in Education*, London: Routledge & Kegan Paul.

Archbishop of Canterbury's Commission (1985) *Faith in the City*, London: Church House Publishing.

Beaudelot, C. and Establet, R. (1971) *L'Ecole Capitaliste en France*, Paris: Maspero.

Beesley, M.F. (1988) 'Practical approaches to spirituality in schools', unpublished MA (Ed.) dissertation, University of Southampton.

Bell, D. (1960) *The End of Ideology: on the Exhaustion of Political Ideas in the Fifties*, Glencoe: Free Press.

Bell, D. (1977) 'The return of the sacred: the argument of the future of religion', *British Journal of Sociology*, 28(4):419–49.

Berger, P.L. (1973) *The Social Reality of Religion*, Harmondsworth: Penguin.

Berger, P.L. (1980) *The Heretical Imperative: Contemporary Possibilities of Religious Affirmation*, London: Collins.

Berger, P.L. and Luckmann, T. (1967) *The Social Construction of Reality: a Treatise in the Sociology of Knowledge*, Harmondsworth: Penguin.

Block, J.H. (ed.) (1971) *Mastery Learning: Theory and Practice*, New York: Holt, Rinehart and Winston.

Bloom, A. (1988) *The Closing of the American Mind*, Harmondsworth: Penguin.

Bohm, D. (1981) *Wholeness and the Implicate Order*, London: Routledge & Kegan Paul.

Bourdieu, P. and Passeron, C. (1977) *Reproduction in Education, Society and Culture*, London: Sage.

Bourne, B., Eichler, U. and Hesman, D. (eds) (1987) *Modernity and its Discontents*, Nottingham: Spokesman.

Bowles, S. and Gintis, H. (1976) *Schooling in Capitalist America: Educational Reform and the Contradictions of Economic Life*, London: Routledge & Kegan Paul.

British Journal of Religious Education (1985) 'Spirituality across the curriculum', 7(3).

Callaghan, J. (1976) 'Towards a national debate', *Education*, 22 October.

Capra, F. (1983) *The Turning Point: Science, Society and the Rising Culture*, London: Fontana.

References

Cochrane,R. and Billig, M. (1982) 'Adolescent support for the National Front: a test of three models of political extremism', *New Community*, 10: 86–94.

Cox, H. (1984) *Religion in the Secular City*, New York: Simon and Schuster.

Craig, M. (1988) *Spark from Heaven: the Mystery of the Madonna of Medjugorje*, London: Hodder & Stoughton.

Crosland, A. (1956) *The Future of Socialism*, London: Cape.

Cupitt, D. (1976) *The Worlds of Science and Religion*, London: Sheldon Press.

Davies, P. (1984) *God and the New Physics*, Harmondsworth: Penguin.

Defois, G. (1982) *L'Occident en Mal d'Espoir*, Paris: Fayard.

Department of Education and Science (1969) *Aspects of Secondary Education in England and Wales*, London: HMSO.

Department of Education and Science (1977) *The Curriculum 11–16: Working Papers by HM Inspectorate: a Contribution to Current Debate*, London: DES.

Department of Education and Science and Welsh Office (1983) *Curriculum 11–16: Towards a Statement of Entitlement*, London: HMSO.

Department of Education and Science (1985a) *Better Schools*, London: DES.

Department of Education and Science (1985b) *The School Curriculum 5 to 16*, London: DES.

Department of Education and Science and Welsh Office (1987) *The National Curriculum 5–16: a Consultation Document*, London: DES.

Dewey, J. (1963) *Experience and Education*, New York: Collier.

Ehrenzweig, A. (1970) *The Hidden Order of Art: a Study in the Psychology of Artistic Imagination*, St Albans: Paladin.

Emler, N.P. and Reicher, S. (1987) 'Adolescent delinquency', in McGurck, H. (ed.) *What Next? an Introduction to Research on Young People*, London: ESRC.

European Community Action Programme (1988) *Transition Education for the 90s: the Experience of the European Community's Action Programme*, Brussels: IFAPLAN.

Felderhof, M.C. (ed.) *Religious Education in a Pluralistic Society*, London: Hodder & Stoughton.

Ferguson, M. (1982) *The Aquarian Conspiracy: Personal and Social Transformation in the 1980s*, London: Granada.

Ferrarotti, F. (1984) *Une Théologie pour Athées*, Paris: Méridiens.

Freire, P. (1972) *Pedagogy of the Oppressed*, Harmondsworth: Penguin.

Freire, P. (1985) *The Politics of Education, Culture, Power and Liberation*, London: Macmillan.

Fromm, E. (1966) *Man for Himself: an Enquiry into the Psychology of Ethics*, New York: Fawcett.

Gattegno, C. (1970) *What We Owe Children: the Subordination of Teaching to Learning*, London: Routledge & Kegan Paul.

Glock, C.Y. and Bellah, R. (1976) *The New Religious Consciousness*, Berkeley: University of California Press.

Grimmitt, M. (1987) *Religious Education and Human Development*, London: McCrimmon.

Groome, T. H. (1980) *Christian Religious Education: Sharing our Story and Vision*, San Francisco: Harper & Row.

Gutierrez, G. (1983) *A Theology of Liberation: History, Politics, Salvation,* London: SCM Press.
Hardy, Sir A. (1979) *The Spiritual Nature of Man,* Oxford: Clarendon Press.
Hargreaves, D.H. (1967) *Social Relations in the Secondary School,* London: Routledge & Kegan Paul.
Hargreaves, D.H. (1982) *The Challenge for the Comprehensive School: Culture, Curriculum and Community,* London: Routledge & Kegan Paul.
Harwood, A.C. (1958) *The Recovery of Man in Childhood: a Study in the Educational Work of Rudolph Steiner,* London: Hodder & Stoughton.
Hay, D. (1985) 'Suspicion of the spiritual: teaching religion in a world of secular experience', *British Journal of Religious Education* 7 (3): 140–7.
Hay, D. (1987) *Exploring Inner Space: Is God Still Possible in the Twentieth Century?,* London: Mowbray.
Hemming, J. (1986) *Instead of God: a Pragmatic Reconsideration of Beliefs and Values,* London: Marion Boyars.
Her Majesty's Inspectorate (1987) *Good Behaviour and Discipline in Schools: a Report,* London: DES.
Hervieu-Léger, D. (1986) *Vers un Nouveau Christianisme,* Paris: Cerf.
Hill, B. (1982) *Faith at the Blackboard: Issues Facing the Christian Teacher,* Grand Rapids, Michigan: Eerdmans.
Hill, B. (1987) *Values Education in Australian Schools,* Perth: Murdoch University School of Education.
Hirst, P. (1985) 'Education and diversity of belief', in Felderhof, M.C. (ed.) *Religious Education in a Pluralistic Society,* London: Hodder & Stoughton, 1985)
Hofstadter, D.R. (1982) 'Prelude...ant fugue', in Hofstadter, D.R. and Dennett, D.C. (eds) *The Mind's I: Fantasies and Reflections on Self and Soul,* Harmondsworth: Penguin.
Holmes, P. (1984) 'Holistic Nursing', *Nursing Times,* 18 April: 28–29.
Hopson, B. and Scally, M. (1981) *Lifeskills Teaching,* London: McGraw-Hill.
Hulmes, E. (1979) *Commitment and Neutrality in Religious Education,* London: Chapman.
Huxley, A. (1980) *The Human Situation,* St Albans: Triad.
Illich, I. (1971) *De-schooling Society,* London: Calder & Boyars.
Independent Commission on International Development Issues (1980) *North–South: a Programme for Survival* (the Brandt Report), London: Pan.
Jaffe, A. (1975) *The Myth of Meaning: Jung and the Expansion of Consciousness,* Harmondsworth: Penguin.
Jaki, S. (1978) *The Road of Science and the Ways to God,* Edinburgh: Scottish Academic Press.
Jones, A. (ed.) (1986) *Making RE More Affective: Twenty Structures for the Classroom,* Nottingham University: Religious Education Research Project.
Joyeux, H. and Laurentin, R. (1987) *Scientific and Medical Studies on the Apparitions at Medjugorje,* Dublin: Veritas.
Jung, C.G. (1933) *Modern Man in Search of his Soul,* London: Harcourt Brace.
Jung, C.G. (1974) *Memories, Dreams, Reflections,* London: Collins.
Kuhn, T. (1970) *The Structure of Scientific Revolutions,* Chicago: University

References

Lacey, C. (1970) *Hightown Grammar*, Manchester: Manchester University Press.
Layton, D. (1986) 'Revaluing science education', in Tomlinson, P. and Quinton, M. (eds) *Values Across the Curriculum*, London: Falmer Press.
Longley, C. (1988) 'The fount of moral indifference', *The Times*, 18 April.
Marcuse, H. (1972) *One-dimensional Man*, London: Abacus.
Maritain, J. (1962) *The Education of Man*, London: Doubleday.
Maritain, J. (1969) *Pour une Philosophie de l'Education*, Paris: Fayard.
Medawar, P.B. (1969) *The Art of the Soluble: Creativity and Originality in Science*, Harmondsworth: Penguin.
Merton, T. (1949) *Elected Silence*, London: Hollis and Carter.
Morgan, I.N. (1988) 'Achieving the intended curriculum in secondary schools', unpublished PhD Dissertation, University of Southampton.
Mourral, I. (1984) *Vous Dites Ecole? La France répond Liberté*, Paris: Latines.
Myrdal, G.(1960) *Beyond the Welfare State*, London: Duckworth.
Newbigin, L. (1986) *Foolishness to the Greeks: the Gospel and Western Culture* London: SPCK.
Newman, J. (1986) *Return to the Sacred: a Socio-Religious Analysis*, Dublin: Four Courts Press.
O'Murchú, D. (1986) *The God Who Became Redundant*, Leominster: Fowler–Wright.
Otto, R. (1923) *The Idea of the Holy: an Enquiry into the Non-Rational Factor in the Idea of the Divine and its Relation to the Rational*, London: Oxford University Press.
Pietroni, P. (1986) *Holistic Living: a Guide to Self-Care*, London: Dent.
Plunkett, D. and Lynch, J. (1973) *Teacher Education and Cultural Change: England, France, West Germany*, London: Allen & Unwin.
Plunkett, D. (1985) 'The timeless and the timely', in Souper, P.C. (ed.) *The Spiritual Dimension of Education*, Southampton: University of Southampton Department of Education.
Plunkett, D. (1986a) 'Vocationalization of the curriculum: the teacher training response in England and France', *Secondary Education Journal* 16(2): 10–12.
Plunkett, D. (1986b) 'Vocational preparation: policy issues in England and Western Europe', in Rist, R.C. (ed.) *Finding Work: Cross-National Perspectives on Employment and Training*, London: Falmer.
Plunkett, D. (1988) 'Defining educational values', *Occasional Paper*, Oxford: Farmington Institute for Christian Studies.
Plunkett, D. (1989) 'Values education and the new RE', *Values* 4 (1): 28.
Plunkett, D. (forthcoming) *Queen of Prophets: the Spiritual Message of Medjugorje*, London: Darton, Longman and Todd.
Porritt, J. (1986) 'The earth in our hands', *The Planet*, London: International Broadcasting Trust.
Post, L. van der (1978) *Jung and the Story of our Time*, Harmondsworth: Penguin.
Priestley, J. (1985) 'The spiritual in the curriculum', in Souper, P.C. (ed.) *The Spiritual Dimension of Education*, Southampton: University of

148

Southampton Department of Education.

Prost, A. (1968) *L'Enseignement en France: 1800–1967*, Paris: Armand Colin.

Robinson, E. (1975) *The Original Vision*, New York: Seabury Press.

Robinson, E. and Jackson, M. (1987) *Religion and Values at Sixteen Plus*, Oxford: Alister Hardy Research Centre.

Rogers, C. (1978) *Carl Rogers on Personal Power*, London: Constable.

Rogers, C. (1983) *Freedom to Learn for the 80s*, Columbus, Ohio: Merrill.

Roszak, T. (1981) *Person/Planet: the Creative Disintegration of Industrial Society*, London: Granada.

Schumacher, E.E. (1974) *Small is Beautiful: a Study of Economics as if People Mattered*, London: Abacus.

Stradling, R., Noctor, M. and Baines, B. (1984) *Teaching Controversial Issues*, London: Edward Arnold.

Teilhard de Chardin, P. (1961) *The Phenomenon of Man*, New York: Harper & Row.

Teilhard de Chardin, P. (1974) *Le Milieu Divin*, Paris: Seuil.

Teilhard de Chardin, P. (1974) *Let me Explain*, London: Fontana.

Teilhard de Chardin, P. (1982) *The Future of Man*, London: Fount.

The Planet (c.1987) London: International Broadcasting Trust.

Tresmontant, C. (1980) *Problèmes du Christianisme*, Paris: Seuil.

Trigg, R. (1973) *Reason and Commitment*, London: Cambridge University Press.

Valadier, P. (1987) *L'Eglise en Procès: Catholicisme et Société Moderne*, Paris: Calmann–Levy.

Waller, W. (1932) *The Sociology of Teaching*, Oxford: Wiley.

Ward, K. (1986) *The Turn of the Tide: Christian Belief in Britain Today*, London: BBC Publications.

Watson, B. (1987) *Education and Belief*, Oxford: Blackwell.

Williams, R. (1961) *The Long Revolution*, Harmondsworth: Penguin.

Willis, P. (1977) *Learning to Labour: How Working Class Kids Get Working Class Jobs*, Farnborough: Saxon House.

Witkin, R.W. (1974) *The Intelligence of Feeling*, London: Holt, Rinehart and Winston.

World Commission on Environment and Development (1987) *Our Common Future* (the Brundtland Report), London: Oxford University Press.

Name Index

Subject Index

Aids 13, 34, 60–1, 91, 101, 123, 130–1

beliefs 4, 7, 90; education and 56; Christian 131; in God 24, 50, 84, 86, 111; Marxism and 57, 60; own 6, 138; in relativism 54; spiritual 21, 22, 52, 108, 117, 124, 138, 139; values and 10, 17, 81, 85–9, 93, 101, 122–3, 125, 127
body 14; mind and 20, 74, 80; mind, spirit and 69, 72, 76, 82, 116, 119, 132; spirit and 108
brain 14, 62, 73, 74

Christian(ity) 23, 45, 81, 89, 114, 116, 117, 123, 139; Christian–Marxist perspective 52; enlightenment and 80; other-worldly 21, 88; schools 97–9; traditional 62; *see also* values
consciousness 66–70, 80, 83, 86; faith and 87–8, 110
consciousness-raising 9, 13, 52, 92
creativity 13, 14, 15, 61, 72, 118, 133, 135; area of learning and experience 54, 56, 58; forces 24; rationality and 114–15; spiritual and 80, 129–30, 135; unconscious and 67, 70
Creator 15, 16, 24, 58, 80, 83, 105
culture 3, 14, 17, 22, 23, 47, 49, 50, 62–3, 87, 131; counter- 10; enterprise 38–9, 113, 127; feminism and 68; of possession 20

cults 22, 63, 69, 76, 88
curriculum 27, 43, 48, 107, 109, 112; -builders 13; centralized control of 31–3; controversial issues 34, 72, 89, 123, 131; core 36, 128; entitlement 35; holistic 72–3, 128; liberal tradition 54–5; Marxism and 51–2; National 5, 28, 29, 32, 34, 36–9, 128; neutral 56, 89; rational 54–5, 58, 99, 110–11, 127; religious schools and 21, 97–9, 110, 125; secular 4; social structure and 50–2; spiritual and 5, 83–4, 95, 96–7, 99–102, 121–32; value change and 130; vocational 31–2, 33–4, 35, 55; whole 73, 74, 98, 125, 128, 132

ecology(ical) 5, 20, 70–6, 77, 110–11; deep 71; feminism and 71
education(al): aims 28, 29, 34, 54, 72, 109, 113, 114, 122, 123, 129, 130; belief and 111; crisis in 10; formal 12; holistic 5, 23, 63, 68, 71–6, 80, 113; industry and 29, 31–3, 40; as investment 35, 129; personal, social and moral 34, 35, 37, 54, 60, 72, 98, 123; policy 29–33, 36, 37, 45, 49–50, 114, 120; purposes 13, 15, 16, 20, 21, 22, 42, 43, 49, 54, 112, 113, 120, 124, 125, 139; rational 23, 45, 49–58, 72, 75; reform 13; Reform Bill/Act 5, 23, 37, 38, 41, 81, 125, 128–9; religious (subject) 54, 89,